SUCCESSFUL
SELLING SKILLS
FOR SMALL BUSINESS

The Small Business Series

DAVID M. BROWNSTONE, *GENERAL EDITOR*

SUCCESSFUL SELLING SKILLS FOR SMALL BUSINESS

David M. Brownstone

A HUDSON GROUP BOOK

David M. Brownstone, *General Editor*

John Wiley & Sons, Inc.
New York   Chichester   Brisbane   Toronto

Library of Congress Cataloging in Publication Data

Brownstone, David M.
   Successful selling skills for small business.

   (Wiley small business series)
   "A Hudson Group book."
   1. Selling. I. Title.
HF5438.25.B76   658.85   77-26835
ISBN 0-471-04029-0

Produced and Designed by Ken Burke & Associates

10 9 8 7 6 5 4 3 2 1

Manufactured in the United States of America

CONTENTS

ONE

Pride and Skill

THE TIME: A COLD SATURDAY AFTERNOON IN JANUARY. IT'S a little before five; the sun has almost set, and the streetlights are on.

The place: The main thoroughfare of a smallish suburban town, located on the outskirts of a major midwestern city.

It's a gray day; snow has been forecast for that night and tomorrow morning, and the first few flakes are beginning to drift down.

Charlie Harris has had a very quiet day in his small furniture store. A lot of time spent "checking stock," a good deal more spent just waiting, a few prospective customers that looked as if they might turn into selling situations and didn't. Altogether, a pretty disappointing day.

His wife had come in to help, as she did every Saturday, but it was apparent by midafternoon that she was not needed. So she'd left, to prepare for the company they were having that night. Charlie usually closed at 5:30 on Saturdays, but today he'd put everything in order and was thinking of closing just a little early this once and starting the ten-mile drive home to beat the coming snowstorm.

As he was starting for the front door, two people came in—a man and a woman, both in their thirties or forties, dressed casually, as people did around town on weekends. They were strangers; that was not surprising—Charlie featured a nationally known line of bedroom furniture that drew people from a fairly wide area.

The man came toward Charlie, looking doubtful, and spoke hesitantly. "Hello."

"Good afternoon." Charlie was polite, not very warm. These people weren't the best prospects he'd ever seen. The woman was still standing just inside the door, hadn't unbuttoned her coat, and was looking around vaguely.

"Anything I can do for you?" He moved past the man, switched off the main window lights, turned to face the man again. He was now standing between the man and the woman— back to the woman.

The woman spoke from behind him. "Oh, we're sorry. You seem to be closing. We were just going to look around a little bit." She sounded tired.

He turned to face her. "No, not really. I'll be here for a little while longer. Is there anything in particular you'd like to see?"

"Well, we thought we might look at some cots or folding beds or something like that."

"Oh. Well, there are some over there. If you see anything you like, let me know. I'll be in the back of the store." He smiled, moved away. No use spending much time with people who just wanted to look at some of the least expensive things in the store. Probably weren't going to buy, anyway. And the snow was beginning to come down a little harder outside. He could see it against the streetlights.

Charlie walked toward the rear of the store, a little troubled, aware that his customers were slowly moving in the direction he'd indicated.

It hit him about halfway to the rear door, which he always carefully rechecked before closing. Had that been Charlie Harris talking back there? He'd always said that when he was so far gone that he was passing up customers, he'd quit, go into some other line of work. And anyway, it was late, they were tired, too, wouldn't be out shopping if they didn't need to do so.

He chuckled. Mind your manners, Charlie; these people are your guests.

Charlie Harris turned, swiftly moved to where the man and woman were standing, took a careful second look at them as he approached.

The woman was probably in her early forties, casually but expensively dressed. The man was a little older, a bit of gray at the temples; he was looking rather carefully at some sleeping bags.

"I'm sorry. I think I could have been more helpful when you walked in a moment ago. I'm Charlie Harris, and this is my place. Now let me put the lights back on so that you can see what you're looking at, and try to be a little more helpful. For openers, wouldn't you both like a cup of coffee? I have some out back, and you both look as if you could use some."

He'd guessed right: got a big smile from the woman and a more reserved, but equally warm smile from the man.

The man held out his hand. "My name is Williams. John Williams. This is my wife, Harriet. You can forget about the coffee, but you really can help us out of a spot.

"I've just been transferred into the area. We've bought a home here, arrived today with our three children, and find that our furniture hasn't come yet. Right now, we're deciding whether to buy some sleeping bags or move into a motel. With the weather the way it is, that furniture may not get here for a few days. Do you have anything to suggest?"

Charlie did indeed have some things to suggest. They left an hour later, after he'd helped them load three top-of-the-line sleeping bags and two good rollaways into the back of their station wagon. They had coffee with him before they left, told him how much they appreciated his help, and swore they'd never buy a piece of furniture again without giving him first chance at the sale.

And they were as good as their word. It turned out that John Williams had been transferred in to build a new department in one of the larger plants in the area. In the next six months, the

Williams family came back for substantial purchases and steered at least a dozen other new arrivals to Charlie.

Charlie Harris is an old pro. But even an old pro can get tired, let other factors get in the way of the sale, do some basic things wrong.

This time, Charlie started by doing almost everything wrong. He was cool; switched off the lights; got between his customers so that his back was to one of them and then turned his back on the other; walked away instead of moving with his customers to show and sell his merchandise. Those were the worst kinds of errors of commission.

His errors of omission were at least as bad. He failed to introduce himself properly and make proper first contact with his customers; didn't make any real effort to size them up; asked no questions aimed at understanding their needs and empathizing with their wants.

He recovered only because he was an old pro, with pride in himself and his business. Charlie Harris had spent many years building that pride, right along with his business. He was accustomed to regarding everyone who came into his store as he would a guest in his home, and had been astonished and dismayed by what he regarded as his own lack of elementary good manners in this situation.

What he did then came very naturally. It was right and it felt good to do it right.

Harriet and John Williams needed help, and they knew it. They were tired, were as dismayed by Charlie's bad manners as he was, and were trying to make the best of it by going ahead to look at his merchandise anyway.

When Charlie came back and started all over again, they were delighted. They needed a friend, and Charlie came through for them.

People remember that sort of thing, far beyond the service rendered. In an increasingly difficult world, small decencies are often appreciated all out of proportion, simply because they sometimes seem so rare.

That's pretty obvious. But the question is—what would you have done on that cold, snowy January evening? Would you have overcome your own depression and negative feeling, reversed your initial mistake, gone back and sized up the situation again, made the sale? Do you have that combination of well-founded self-confidence, pride in your own business, and seasoned selling skills that characterizes the most successful small business owners?

A further question—would one of your employees, or for that matter a family member working in the store, have done the right thing in this situation, and made the sale? Just how highly motivated and well trained are the other people selling your goods?

That's what this book is about—motivation and selling skills. They go hand in hand. Eager, highly motivated people often make basic selling errors, keep on doing so simply because they've never had the benefit of any training in the basics of selling, in seeing, listening, sizing up a selling situation, making the simple, right basic moves that result in sales. Conversely, we have all seen highly trained salespeople who are listless, "sour," turn away potential customers. Motivation gone, the best trained salespeople in the world are duds.

This book points up that combination of high motivation and good basic skills which results in consistently successful selling.

TWO

Sell Benefits

*Identifying Customer Benefits / Mistaking Features
for Benefits / Puffs*

W HAT ARE YOU SELLING?
  On the face of it, that's a pretty foolish question. If
you're in the grocery business, you sell groceries. If you run a
restaurant, you sell meals. Furniture stores sell furniture. It
seems obvious.

But put the same question differently.

*What are your customers buying when they buy whatever
you're selling?*

Very simply and basically put, they're buying *benefits*—what
they think your product or service will do for them.

When you sell washing machines, isn't the main thing to know
what you're selling and to be able to demonstrate the superior
qualities of your machines?

No. That's not the main thing. The main thing is to show the
customer how the washer will save time and clean better. Of
course, you must be able to describe the superior qualities of
your washer, *but always in terms of the benefits the customer
will gain, what your goods will do for your customer.*

Not long ago, the author was in the market for a good small
electronic calculator. He went out to buy one several times. Each

time, he was met by a seller who carefully, precisely, and glowingly described the features of the calculators being shown. He heard all about miniaturization, memories, floating decimals, logarithmic functions; very little about what each calculator might do for him.

Ultimately, he ran into a seller who asked him what sort of work he did, what kinds of calculations he hoped to be able to do. That seller listened, really listened, asked a few questions about whether or not some other functions might or might not be useful, nodded, pulled out a little calculator that had programmed into it a few very basic business calculation functions, briefly demonstrated how it worked, and made a sale. It took about fifteen minutes, from start to finish. There was hardly any "technical talk" between seller and customer. The customer was shown how to achieve his goals by use of the calculator shown, and he bought. Of course, the features of the calculator were demonstrated, but always within the context of satisfaction of the customer's needs; within the context of the *benefits* the customer would get from the calculator.

The calculator purchase illuminated several of the most basic approaches to successful selling:

- Note first that the seller *listened.* Check those who sell your goods to see how well they listen to their customers.
- Then the seller *asked some questions,* to better understand the felt needs of the customer, perhaps to be able to suggest some benefits the customer might get from the calculator that the customer hadn't thought of.
- With needs firmly in mind, and with the customer fully involved in the "selling process" by then, the seller was able to *identify wants and needs, demonstrate,* and *sell* the calculator (a somewhat more expensive one than the customer had in mind, by the way).
- The calculator demonstration was brief, directed to the identified needs of the customer, and therefore entirely successful. In fact, the seller was entirely confident in her handling of the calculator, and didn't have to fall back on the jargon the customer had encountered in other stores. The seller demonstrated every important (*important to the*

customer, that is) feature of the calculator, relating each feature to the identified needs of the customer, thus *converting the features of the calculator into benefits to the customer.*

We will return to that idea again and again. To be able to convert product features into customer benefits is central to successful selling. That means that you must be able to develop information that will help you understand the customer's needs and make yourself thereby able to sell your goods and services to those needs.

IDENTIFYING CUSTOMER BENEFITS

A middle-aged man came into an outdoor and garden store and asked to look at lawn mowers. The seller showed him the whole line, from the most expensive sit-down garden tractors costing a couple of thousand dollars to the least expensive mowers, hand-propelled, selling for $49.50. After about an hour the customer left, unsold, leaving a puzzled seller behind, wondering where things had gone wrong.

Sometimes a seller wishes it were possible to go along invisibly with the unsold prospect into several other situations, to see what the customer eventually buys and why. If that puzzled lawn-mower seller could have done so, he would have witnessed something like this.

"Good morning. Can I help you?" The speaker is Jimmy Walton, a college student working part-time on Saturday mornings in his family's outdoor and garden store.

"Hello. I'd like to look at some lawn mowers," responds Ken Warren, the same middle-aged man.

"Surely. If you'll step over here, I'll show you our line of lawn equipment." They walk toward the rear of the store and stop in an area containing a wide variety of machines and tools to work the ground.

"Perhaps I can be of some help if I know a little about the kind of job your lawn mower has to do. How much lawn do you have to cut?" Jimmy asks.

"Well, it's not very big. It's just the front lawn and a little around the sides and back of the house." Ken looks at the smallest of the sit-down tractors, turns over the price tag, and frowns when he sees that it costs a little over $800. He walks toward one of the smaller motorized mowers, stops and looks indecisive.

"Sometimes a little bit of lawn can be a lot of mowing, though," Jimmy says. "Is your land the kind of up-hill-and-down-dale property we seem to specialize in around here?"

"It sure is." Ken smiles ruefully. "And I'm getting a little tired of pushing a lawn mower uphill. But I can't quite see spending a lot of money for a tractor, either."

"Well, maybe you don't have to spend a lot of money to get the job done. Have you considered a self-propelled mower? We sell quite a lot of them for just the kind of situation you're describing. Take this model over here. It has a 20-inch cut, plenty of power, and will pull itself right uphill, with you walking behind to guide it. All you have to do is set the walking speed most convenient for you and go for a walk around your property."

No need to carry the conversation further here. Jimmy has made the sale. He made a good first impression, asked a couple of basic right questions, and really listened to the answers to those questions. Then, with the information developed, he was able to move in and push exactly the right button. The lawn mower's feature is that it is self-propelled; its benefit is that Ken wouldn't have to push it uphill. Price was not an issue here, as Ken was even considering a much higher-priced tractor to solve the problem, but really hadn't been able to justify the price.

Should Jimmy have tried to sell Ken a tractor? Certainly not. He'd seen Ken look at his lowest-priced tractor and turn away, and it was clear that the self-propelled mower would do the job. Jimmy questioned, listened, developed information, found the right feature, converted it into the crucial customer benefit, and made the sale.

MISTAKING FEATURES FOR BENEFITS

Often, features are so widely advertised and discussed that it's easy to mistake a feature for a benefit.

Take for example the automobile salesman who tells all comers that the little foreign car he's selling gets 30 miles to a gallon of gasoline. He honestly thinks he's selling an extraordinary benefit; his prospects react well; his car's advertising stresses the 30-miles-to-a-gallon feature.

And it's a great feature, if true. But it's a feature, not a benefit. How much stronger the selling presentation will be if 30 miles per gallon is translated into cash savings!

The benefit is that if you drive 15,000 miles per year in your present car, which gets 15 miles per gallon, you use 1,000 gallons a year. In the little foreign car, you would use 500 gallons. That's 500 gallons of gas a year that you would save. At 65¢ per gallon, you would save $325 a year—every year. That's tangible. That's a benefit.

Equally often, features are mistaken for benefits because sellers do not have a firm understanding of what is a feature and what is a benefit.

Often the problem is compounded by customers who describe their wants and needs in terms of features. The customer who says "I'm in the market for a good heavy-duty electric sander" is likely to be shown just that by a seller who then goes ahead to demonstrate all the heavy-duty aspects of the sander, never realizing that more information is needed, that the customer's description has to be translated into benefits before the sale is likely to be made.

What the customer is probably saying is "I'm about to do some work that involves sanding. I think it requires a big, heavy sander to do the job." He may also be thinking "I hope it doesn't cost more than I'm willing to spend." The seller needs to ask what kinds of jobs the sander is needed for, and may indeed find that the customer's work and pocketbook needs will be well satisfied by what the seller thinks of as a good lightweight, medium-priced sander.

The key to keeping features and benefits properly identified lies in continually asking the question "What will this product do for this customer?" What it does for the customer is the benefit; what it does, how it's operated, what it's made of, how it's made—all else about it—are features.

Putting it a little differently, a benefit somehow satisfies a customer's need or want; a feature is an aspect of the product.

It can be a comparative aspect and still be a feature, not a benefit. That a product is "less expensive" is a comparative feature of the product. That it "saves money" is the benefit.

When your product is "better made" than any of its competitors, that's a feature. That "it will save you a lot of money in the long run because it's so well made" is the benefit.

PUFFS

"Mrs. Smith, that's far and away the best set of silverware we have in the store. And it's a marvelous value besides."

Best for whom? Value for whom? Is Mrs. Smith convinced that the silverware looks beautiful, will look beautiful in her home? Will she somehow save money because of the "value" of the silverware? How?

Beware the "puff," the seemingly unsupported exaggeration. There's nothing like it to destroy your credibility and turn a promising selling situation into a lost sale.

The seeming exaggeration often occurs when a seller stresses benefits without first laying the necessary groundwork in terms of the features of the product.

Sell benefits, but don't neglect features. Features, fully explained and satisfactorily proven, provide the basis for believable benefits.

That doesn't mean that it's wrong to put the benefits first. "This is our finest lightweight sander. You'll get years of trouble-free use out of it. It's so well built and so durable that the manufacturers have put a two-year guarantee on it. Let me show you just how well built it is, and some of the ways you'll be able to make use of it."

But if all the same seller had said was "This is our finest lightweight sander. You'll get years of trouble-free use out of it," the customer would have had every reason to regard the seller skeptically. And it takes no more than that to finish the sale before it's fairly started.

THREE
The Answer Man

The Main Edge I Have Is Me / Getting Product Knowledge

J OE FORD IS AN ANSWER MAN.
Six years ago, Joe opened a hardware store in a small shopping plaza located in a little town outside a major northeastern
city.

There was and is a somewhat larger shopping plaza across the
road, with a supermarket that sells some hardware items, a
bank, and several small stores.

Not more than ten-minutes' drive away are two much larger
shopping plazas, each with its own major department store,
complete with discount hardware department. In addition, there
are large, well-established hardware stores within the same ten-
minute driving radius, all of which carry full stocks of hardware
and garden and home materials at prices comparable to Joe's.

Joe had been a carpenter and jack-of-all trades around the
home-building industry before he went into the hardware business. Actually, it was the downturn in new home construction
that made him think about going into business for himself. And,
like many another aspiring small business owner, he did it with
his savings, some money borrowed from relatives, and a not-
very-large bank loan secured by his own personal assets.

13

The first six months were the hardest. But then the word began to get around that Joe knew what he was doing, that although some of his prices were a little higher than the discount stores', you could be sure you'd be getting the right tool, the right paint remover, the right widget when you didn't even know which widget to ask for. All you had to do was to describe what it was you were trying to accomplish, and nine times out of ten Joe would know what to recommend. Sometimes you had to wait a little while while Joe prescribed for someone else. But it beat driving to the department store, wandering around in the hardware department, and finally getting something you thought might do the job, only to find when you got home that it wouldn't—and then back to the department store.

Joe is a nice guy. He greets everyone who comes into his store with the same friendly and polite "Good day, can I help you?" after letting them get their bearings. He lets the browsers browse and answers the questions of those seeking help, loud and clear enough for the browsers to hear that good help is being sold as well as hardware. He answers every question as best he can and treats no one brusquely, even those asking the most elementary questions for the third time.

It's not an act. Joe really enjoys helping people solve their problems. And people enjoy doing business with him. Many of his customers pass up lower-priced home equipment in the supermarket across the road to buy Joe's slightly higher-priced mops, brooms, and brushes, because they know that if Joe sells them something, somehow it's going to suit them better.

Joe sells a lot of items that aren't strictly hardware these days. After his lean first six months, and twelve months beyond that were just about break-even, he began to do better and better. After his third year, he took over the shop next door, vacated by a retiring grocer. Last year, he took over the shop on the other side, so that he could put in some new departments.

His customers still come in and ask him how to repair leaky faucets; they stay to buy paint, blenders, and snow blowers. Partly because they trust Joe Ford. Partly because Joe Ford is a very fine salesman.

Joe knows the secret of his success.

"I like people and I like working hard. Before I decided to go into this business, I figured the way to make it was to get to know everything I could about the business, the stock, the customers. I haunted the department stores, tried to size up their strengths and weaknesses. Got a job weekends selling in a hardware store, to learn something about the trade—how a little guy like me could compete, with the double disadvantage of higher prices and less stock.

"Finally, I figured the main edge I had was me. I was older, more experienced, had more incentive than the clerks in the department stores. And I figured I could go head-to-head with the other hardware stores around here, because I was willing to learn everything there was to learn about my stock, and keep my patience with the customers besides, which is what a lot of hardware store owners forget to do.

"So I studied. All the materials I could find. The manuals, the manufacturers' brochures; I buttonholed my suppliers and pumped them dry about the goods they were selling me. And I welcomed the customer's questions. During that first pretty lean year and a half, I did a lot more than get a good reputation around here. What I did was to learn by doing. Every time I solved a customer's problem, I learned how to solve the same problem for other customers. After a while, it looked to them as if I was a whiz. They never stopped to think that I'd had the same question asked a dozen times in the last few months.

"And I kept my patience. It helps that I really do like people—most people, anyway—and kind of automatically put myself into their shoes when they come to me with a question."

THE MAIN EDGE I HAVE IS ME

Sales professionals often look down their collective noses at retail selling. Much of the accepted wisdom among sellers, managers, and trainers is that retail selling is the lowest kind of selling, fit only for those who "can't make it" in outside selling.

That view of retail selling has grown up since the advent of the big department store, the discount store, the basically self-service store, and the supermarket. In those kinds of retail operations, the stress is on low prices and high volume, with as little as possible budgeted for selling and service. That's the basic reason we often see discount stores with not enough personnel, and half-trained personnel at that. It's not unusual to spend fifteen minutes searching for an item in a discount store and not find anyone to help you; equally common to find that store personnel know very little about their stock. And then to spend ten minutes in a check-out line, while a nice, young, inexperienced, very poorly trained cashier gamely tries to cope with a complicated combination cash register and inventory-recording machine while you wait . . . and wait.

The truth is that there are tens of thousands of highly skilled, motivated professionals in retail selling. They are to be found among the hundreds of thousands of small business owners. And there are tens of thousands more who are in the process of learning by doing—who are teaching themselves how to sell as they run their businesses.

High-quality small business owners are often much like Joe Ford. They tend to know everything they can about their businesses, and especially about the stock they carry. To regard every customer contact as an opportunity to help someone else, and while doing so to make a sale. They tend to place high values upon their own integrity and the integrity of their businesses.

The hardware store owner who is an answer man is a widely observed phenomenon in American business.

So is the beauty shop owner who is an answer woman, who carefully and considerately helps her clients to solve their hair care and other problems; answers their questions patiently and clearly, often steering them away from quite literally harmful products and techniques.

So is the specialty food store owner who really knows cheeses, helps customers try new ones, tactfully steers them away from cheeses they probably won't like, suggests the right crackers and breads to go with the cheeses they've just bought.

Or the liquor store owner who has taken the trouble to become something of an expert on wines, and has opened up a whole new growth area for the store.

Or the independent insurance agent who keeps up with the latest developments in the field, regularly goes to seminars and meetings, studies the material supplied by the insurance companies, and is thus able to help clients get the best possible coverages at the lowest possible costs.

And many of them are solid selling professionals, who use their product knowledge—for that's what we're talking about—as an essential element of their selling success.

GETTING PRODUCT KNOWLEDGE

Joe Ford has the right basic idea. There is no better way to get product knowledge, and in fact knowledge about the business of your choice, than to work in the business.

For the beginner, working in someone else's business is invaluable. You begin to know the stock, the kinds of questions customers raise, and how to handle both the questions and the customers. You begin to know something about how to buy, and how to sell—the management side of the business.

The alert, experienced small business owner always has a lot to keep up with, to learn and relearn. There are several ways to do so:

- *Your customers.* Like Joe Ford, you will learn things from your customers that you simply can't learn anywhere else—what wants and needs they hope to satisfy with your products, how your products are being used, what their benefits and problems are in actual use, and when different products appear in the marketplace that seem to satisfy wants and needs better.
- *Manufacturers' and suppliers' printed materials.* You can get a great deal of product knowledge by reading brochures, manuals, the "how to use" and "how to assemble" instructions that come with some products, and any other printed materials available from manufacturers and other suppliers. The brochure material can often be especially helpful in supplying effective selling approaches, in anticipating common objections and showing how to handle them, and in providing "words of art"—that is, selling language that has proven widely successful in advertising and otherwise promoting the product.

- *Your sales representatives.* Most small businesses have a substantial number of sales representatives calling on them, to get reorders on existing items in stock, to sell new items in existing lines, to attempt to open up new accounts.

  Talk to those sales representatives as much as possible. They can and should be a mine of useful information and selling approaches for the products they represent. They want you to successfully sell their products, and will often extend themselves to try to show you ways to do so, all the way from providing special point-of-sale displays to telling you how others have successfully sold their goods.

  Treat them in the friendliest possible fashion—without, of course, encouraging those few who are time-wasters to waste your time as well as their own. Often a cup of coffee supplied to a tired salesman, late on what has been a quiet day for both of you, can provide you with dividends far beyond your expectations, in terms of selling ideas and selling tools.

- *Trade shows and business meetings.* Try to attend as many trade shows and business meetings as is reasonably possible. There are often new products, new ideas on how to sell old products, new adaptations of all kinds to be aware of and use in your business.

- *Your trade association.* Belong to it if possible, even if you are one of the smallest businesses in it. Of course, sometimes trade associations effectively exclude smaller businesses, due to their focus on the problems and needs of the larger businesses in the industry; and sometimes the dues structure reflects that preoccupation, with dues set far too high for the smaller businesses. But most associations have some useful materials for small business, and there is usually some way to get those materials without too much cost.

  There are often other small business groups, both local and national, you can benefit from joining. Some publish newsletters, manuals, and other materials of value to you in your search for product knowledge and successful selling approaches.

- *Subscribe to an industry magazine.* Here too you may run into a focus on the bigger businesses in the industry, but publishers want to sell their magazines, and you will usually find that one or another magazine serving your industry takes up matters of value to you. Your association can be helpful in recommending the proper publications for you, as can some of your sales representatives.

• *Go to school.* Very often, an adult education course in your community or an evening course at a local college can be tremendously useful in helping you understand some of the basics about how the products you sell work. Then many other materials, such as those supplied by manufacturers, become far more understandable and usable in developing successful selling approaches.

You must know your products inside-out to be able to consistently convert features into customer benefits. Sound product knowledge is basic to selling success.

FOUR

Appearances Matter

When the Selling Process Begins / First Impressions Count

“I 'M NOT OUT TO WIN A MENTION IN *HOUSE BEAUTIFUL,* OR to place in the ten best-dressed bankrupt businessmen contest. I'm here to sell first-class goods at bargain prices, and I'm doing okay, thank you.”

The speaker is George West, a man in his early thirties. Three months earlier, George had taken a short-term lease on a medium-sized warehouse building just across the road from a large, well-established shopping center. The shopping center had had a big W. T. Grant store, which was closed four months ago when the parent company went bankrupt. George sized up the situation, properly realized that there was no comparable store nearby, and set out to snap up some of those “floating” former Grant customers. He had worked for Grant, quit when he saw the handwriting on the wall, and was now running a “bare-bones” operation, with considerable discontinued lot buying, a very small workforce for the size of the operation, and very low rent. Everyone, including George, pitched in to do both warehouse work and selling. He was indeed able to offer some very good buys on the limited selection of goods he stocked. And people had been coming in to buy. It looked as if George had the makings of a good, solid, discount-selling operation.

A year later he was out of business.

No, it wasn't lack of financing that sunk him. Nor competition. Nor lack of variety in the goods offered. Nor working at too thin a margin.

It was simpler than that. George and his store were a mess— dirty, cluttered, uninviting. Eventually, even at bargain prices, people stopped coming in.

The problem was that George had badly underestimated the impact of appearances. It's not so much that people don't buy in the kind of operation he ran because of the way the place looks; it's that they stay away when they think of a place as dirty, uncomfortable, cluttered.

George had always laughed at the very few prospective customers who would come in, look around, and go right out again. "Let them pay higher prices somewhere else," he said. But he hadn't realized they were just the tip of the iceberg, and represented the kind of reaction that would ultimately drive him out of business.

The problem could have been solved easily and inexpensively. George could have hired some part-time help to do a good deal of the warehousing, handled the housekeeping chores with the people he had plus the part-timers, and never felt the small additional costs. And he could himself have sold and supervised, rather than trying to set an example to his staff by doing every kind of job himself, including the hot and dirty ones.

WHEN THE SELLING PROCESS BEGINS

The selling process begins for many prospective customers long before they enter your place of business. It starts with "word of mouth," with advertising seen, with a glimpse of a storefront while driving by, or a browse in your window while taking a walk.

Try to put yourself in the shoes of someone approaching your business for the first time. Go outside, walk a little distance away, turn and approach. What do you see?

Is your walkway swept and clean? If you have any sort of illuminated sign, is it brightly and uniformly lit? (Far better to turn your sign off than to have it on partly lit.)

Getting closer, how's your outside? If you have a window, it should always be clean. Are your doors in good repair and clean?

Stop in front of the window and look in. How does it look from the outside looking in? You're so close to your business that it's awfully hard to "distance" yourself, to see yourself and your business as strangers see you. But do it—it's well worth the effort.

What about the contents of the window display—are they clean, well lit, appealingly laid out?

Look in past the window. There should be people in sight who might help you if you had a question. They should be decently dressed, clean-looking, pleasant and at ease rather than tense and restless.

If there are any customers in sight, they ought to be attended, not looking around for someone to help them.

How's the clutter situation? Boxes should not be left partly opened out on the selling floor. Stains and spills should be cleaned as soon as they happen; papers and dust should be swept often.

Remember the first time you walked into a hotel or motel bedroom that hadn't been made up? You wanted to walk right out again, didn't you? Does your place of business, which you think of as homey and appealing, have all the charm of an unmade bed?

The selling process begins in earnest when you go in the door.

Go through your own front door, still in the shoes of a perfect stranger, going in for the first time. Try to develop a snap first impression. It's important; others do.

Do you see a clean, light, uncluttered, airy place full of life and color? Or a dark, crowded, not very clean, dull, dingy, dead place?

How do the people working there really look? Is the young man approaching you calm, warm, friendly, reasonably well and cleanly dressed? Or did he forget to wipe his boots when he came in out of the rain after lunch, and does his hair look as if it hadn't been combed for a month? Is his mouth curled in what he thinks is a cool and friendly manner, which others interpret as a perpetual sneer?

Walk to a mirror. Look at yourself in the same way you've just looked at the young man. Critically, very critically. Take a personal appearance inventory. Hair should be combed—nails tended—hands clean—shoes clean and not too worn. Remember, people look at the extremities first, form their snap impressions from such seeming trivia as hands, shoes, hair.

Are your clothes right? They should be fairly neutral, rather than flamboyant. No need to dress expensively, but your clothes must be clean and in good repair. You want to sell the benefits your goods convey to your customers, not divert their attention in any way by your appearance or manner.

And what about the first impression your own personality conveys? That person in the mirror should be reasonably calm and friendly-looking, not nervous, drawn, someone you'd just as soon not have sit beside you on a crowded bus.

FIRST IMPRESSIONS COUNT

The fact is that appearances matter a great deal. You and your business have to make a good first impression, continue to make a good impression as long as you're in business.

Customers like coming into a clean, light, friendly place and dealing with warm and decent people. They open up, are receptive, want to buy from you. They don't like coming into places that make them uncomfortable, dealing with people who make them uneasy. You may have the best values in town, but you'd better have an attractive place of business, too, if you want to maintain and grow a successful business.

Total Communication

"S HE'S A GOOD TALKER."
"He talks with his hands."
"I don't like going in there. That man's too stiff-necked for me."
"Did you see how she looked when I told her the guy across the street was underselling her?"

In recent years, books on "communication" have poured off the nation's printing presses by the score—books on "body language," "empathy," and a host of other more or less useful ways of describing what sales professionals have known for a long time.

And not just sales professionals. Everyone involved with convincing and moving other human beings knows that "It's not what you say, but how you say it," and that "You have to be able to put yourself in the other guy's shoes."

In a very real sense, what all the books and articles on communications have done is to rediscover the wheel.

To sell successfully, you must pay a great deal of attention to the plain fact that when you communicate with someone else, you are communicating not only verbally, but in a number of other ways as well.

BODY LANGUAGE

Amy Powell opened a fine little jewelry shop in a medium-sized southwestern city last year. She'd majored in art history in college and then married, had children, and dropped out of the job market. Now that her children were grown, she'd decided to go back to work, in her own business, the kind of business she'd always wanted to own.

She did it right. She worked in someone else's place for a while, started with enough capital, and therefore enough stock, to be able to offer a wide range of price and quality, including a line of beautiful Indian jewelry, handcrafted locally. She had a feel for the jewelry, pretty well knew what her customers wanted, was able to help them select those pieces that best complemented their style, coloring, taste.

Now, after nine months, she was beginning to wonder if she'd made the right choice. Too many prospective customers were coming in, admiring the jewelry, and walking out without buying.

She was talking about it with her oldest daughter one morning at breakfast, before she opened the shop and her daughter headed for her job as a buyer for a local department store.

"I know I'm doing something wrong, Jan. I thought it might be my prices, but my suppliers assure me that my prices are in line with everyone else in town, and I've checked around a little and it's true.

"It's not that the business is so new, either. After nine months, I should be beginning to get some repeat business from satisfied customers. There's some, but not as much as there ought to be. The truth is, I'm stumped."

Jan laughed. "Sounds like b.o., Mom."

Amy looked grim. "I've thought about that, too." She suddenly seemed a good deal older. The store meant a lot to her.

Contrite, Jan had a suggestion. "Look, Mom, I know you about as well as anyone else. Suppose I come in on Saturday and just watch your operation for a while. I won't wait on any customers, just make believe I'm checking stock while I try to see what's happening. It can't do any harm."

Amy agreed, and so the two women spent Saturday afternoon together in the shop. They closed at six and went out for an early dinner.

Jan studied her mother, looking a little puzzled, while Amy studied the menu. Amy smiled, put down the menu, and took off her glasses. "Guess it didn't work, did it, Jan? Well, it was a good try, and thank you very much for trying. It was kind of you to give me your Saturday afternoon."

Jan, still looking at her mother, scratched her ear reflectively. "Not so fast, Mom. Do me a favor, will you? Pick up the menu again, but don't put your glasses on."

"Oh, Jan, you know I'll have a hard time reading it that way." Then, seeing Jan's look, "Okay, okay, anything in the interest of science." She picked up the menu and held it further away, narrowing her eyes and reading it with difficulty.

Jan watched a moment more, began to laugh, and stopped. She reached into her bag, pulled out a small hand mirror, and handed it to Amy. "Try to keep on reading the menu, holding the mirror in the same hand as the menu. Then, without changing the expression on your face, look in the mirror."

Amy did as Jan had requested, drew a blank. She did it again, began to get a glimmer of understanding, and looked across at Jan. She did it a third time, began to laugh herself, and stopped and shook her head.

"Vanity, vanity. I don't wear my glasses in the shop because I think they somehow make me look less smart, less chic. Do I really scowl at the customers when I think I'm concentrating on their needs?"

Jan nodded, very soberly. "You do indeed. At least four times this afternoon, you showed lovely things, watched prospective customers put them on, and scowled fiercely at them while you told them the pieces looked great. To make it worse, you're so near-sighted you couldn't even see their reactions, which were in all cases pure confusion. They couldn't quite believe you were simply lying to make the sale, but also couldn't believe you really meant what you were saying.

"Mom, what you're doing is communicating two mutually contradictory things at once. It's not uncommon, but in selling it's a disaster. We see it in the department store business all the time, and it's one of the hardest things to combat in sales training.

"Wear your glasses in the store, and forget about your vanity. I think you'll find that business improves a great deal."

Amy Powell took her daughter's advice and found that her sales results improved dramatically. And there were two other interesting side effects as well: She could study her customer's reactions a great deal better and adjust her selling approaches to those reactions; and she felt a lot less tired after a day's work. Tension breeds exhaustion, and she hadn't realized just how tense her business situation was making her.

You talk with your whole body. There's nothing wrong with that—we all do. It's as natural as breathing or walking.

That's one of the reasons two people who have lived together for a long time seem to anticipate each other's thoughts and comments. Before one seems even to begin to say something, the other starts to nod, move, somehow begins to communicate a reaction. Often an outsider has the feeling that a whole conversation has taken place within a moment, with the outsider entirely unable to perceive what the conversation was about or how it was conducted.

What happens is that one senses a change in the attitude of the other by the set of the body, an almost inperceptible tilt forward, a slight tensing, a very small movement of head or shoulder. The other responds in kind, an unspoken dialogue follows, and much is resolved before anyone says a word.

You and your customers have the same kind of communication, although of course you don't know each other very well, and are not as able to see some of the more subtle attitude indicators.

In your own environment, though, you can often learn a great deal about your customers through keen observation of their unconscious communications. That's true in the early stages of the selling process, and even more true when you are face to face. You are in your own place, selling products you have sold many times before; you know what reactions to look for and can learn much of what you'll need to know to make the sale from the way your customer's body reacts to your presentation. You'll be looking for tiny nods or disagreements, a thoughtful look when you've touched on a real need or want, a small start of recognition when you've answered a question before it was asked, forestalled an objection before it could be voiced.

Customers also get a great deal from the way you communicate without words. We learn as children to judge how well people like us by watching how they behave toward us rather than listening to what they say. The set of your body, your tensions and relaxations, how you move, whether you really listen or only seem to listen, whether you're being really patient and attentive or faking to cover impatience and boredom, are all conveyed far more through your nonverbal communication to the customer than by your verbal communication. The best selling words in the world are worthless if they are accompanied by poor attitudes.

STIFFNESS

One of the worst selling errors you can make is to try not to talk with your body.

Try it in a full-length mirror. Talk to an imaginary customer about one of your products. Sell it. At the same time, try to keep your body immobile, head and eyes straight ahead.

It's harder to do than it seems. It also makes you look as if you're made of wood. You wouldn't do it with a real live customer in a million years.

Or would you? The exercise above may only be an exaggeration of some very "normal" things you do quite unconsciously.

Many of us like to preserve our privacy to some degree while meeting the public all day. Others are concerned about seeming to overwhelm, to "hard-sell" customers and drive them away. Some of us are simply unsure of how to handle contact with strangers, perhaps a little wary.

Whatever the reasons, the quite normal result of holding back with your customers is that you give them the impression that you are standoffish, stiff-necked, arrogant, distant, cold, don't like them, wish you were somewhere else.

That kind of impression is often heightened by some of the normal body moves that accompany your state of mind. People who are uneasy with customers often stand too straight, move too quickly, seem a little uncoordinated or somewhat tense and nervous, often complicate matters with a bright and clearly artificial smile.

Some people fold their arms. Go to the mirror and study the attitude you convey if you're an arm-folder. Those folded arms are a tangible barrier between you and your customer.

There are those who come to the end of each day headachy, with neck and back aches. That is often simply the effect of the tensions felt while dealing with people, mostly customers. Like the arm-folder, the literally stiff-necked seller needs to change the basic attitude behind the physical symptom. Not at all incidentally, the emotional and physical benefits of doing so are substantial. What you do for a living should not and need not cause you these kinds of difficulties. Loosening-up exercises can be done to minimize the physical effects. And emotional loosening up to get at root causes—that's harder, but indispensible in the long run.

BE OPEN AND NATURAL

The best way to handle customer communications is to let an open and natural style develop.

That means not being afraid to talk, move, gesture as you normally do with friends and family.

If you normally gesture with one or both hands to make a certain kind of point, by all means do so with your customers. Unless you're the kind of excitable, dominating person who makes friends and family nervous, too, the customer won't mind. But don't overdo it, any more than you would with anyone else. The worst error you can make is to try to radically change your natural style of communication. Just amend your natural moves a little, to take into account the wide variety of people you encounter in business. And people immediately sense it when you're trying to be something you're not, and think you're a "phony."

Move freely and easily. If you're walking with a customer, or moving around demonstrating a product, handle yourself as if you were dealing with a friend. It is not at all attractive when a woman moves with little mincing steps, or when a man stands very stiffly erect. If you convey easiness by the way you hold your body, your customer will be reassured and will respond positively to your ease and confidence. Let yourself be friendly. Oh, the occasional customer will be insecure enough to think you're just "putting it on" to make the sale. But if you are able to like people, to expect them to be at their best if you are at your best with them, then most people will see that your warmth is genuine and will respond in kind.

Openness and warmth are conveyed far more by "body language" and tone than by words. "It's not what you say but how you say it" is often quite literally correct.

KEEP YOUR DISTANCE

A word of caution is in order. Be careful of *where* you say it from.

Americans come from scores of different backgrounds, with expressive styles originating in all the diverse cultures of the world. In some cultures, several feet is considered a proper distance between those speaking to each other, while in others, as little as six inches is regarded as entirely acceptable.

That can and does often lead to misunderstandings when people meet in the marketplace—as for instance, in your place of business. It's one of the few areas in which it is not always such a good idea to communicate as you normally do with family and friends.

"I can't stand going into that place. That man is so pushy. He's forever getting up close and waving his hands in my face." Pushy? Not really. Just a store owner with a background different from yours, trying to sell his goods. He moves to what he thinks of as a proper speaking distance, and you back away. Without thinking about it, he immediately moves closer, to re-establish proper distance. The net effect is like a Marx Bros. comedy, with him playing Groucho and chasing you around the store as you back-pedal.

It can work the other way, too, with the seller feeling crowded and losing composure, the thread of the presentation, and ultimately the sale.

VOICE AND DICTION

"There's nothing wrong with my voice!" Those were the famous last words of all those great silent movie stars whose movie careers abruptly ended with the advent of sound.

Nothing really was wrong with their voices—for talking with friends or for ordering food in restaurants. But for leading roles in movies, it's not appropriate to have a robust leading man with a thin, almost falsetto voice; a sultry leading lady who speaks in a little-girl simper.

To sell effectively, you need not have voice and diction suitable for the stage. You do have to be able to make yourself heard, to speak at moderate speed, with clarity, in a voice that is pleasant to the ear of your customer.

There's nothing really "wrong" with your voice if you talk fast, in a high, shrill monotone. The trouble is that most people will find that kind of voice offensive and won't really listen to what it has to say in a selling situation. You may have the best product in the world, but if you turn customers away with the quality and tone of your voice, you won't sell it.

It's hard to know about your own voice. You've lived with it all your life, gotten used to it. You don't really know how it sounds to others.

But others will tell about your voice if you ask, and if they're convinced you'll really listen to what they have to say. Ask those closest to you if your voice is shrill, has a whine in it, is too soft or too loud. Ask whether you speak too slowly, too fast, mumble, have a faint stutter or hesitation have a regional, national, or ethnic accent that makes it hard for your customers to understand you.

And if they tell you there are voice problems, by all means try to correct them.

Practice reading into a mirror or to an obliging family member or friend. Reading aloud is a very good way of slowing down and speaking more clearly—problems that are often related.

There are organizations, like local drama groups and public speaking clubs, which have among their aims the improvement of the verbal skills of their members. You can take public speaking and interpretive reading courses, often in local adult education programs, and may achieve excellent results surprisingly quickly.

Voice and diction are essential selling tools, and can be enormously improved with a little sustained work.

SIX

Listening

Questioning / Put Yourself in the Other Guy's Shoes

TRY THIS EXPERIMENT. IN A BIG ROOM SEAT FIFTEEN OR more people, roughly in a circle. Let a general conversation develop.

Then, during a lull in the conversation, whisper something in the ear of the person to your right, something like "There may be a snowstorm day after tomorrow. Pass that message to the person to your right, and say 'Pass it on to the person on your right.'"

Watch that message make its way around the room, ultimately to come back to you from the person on your left. Listen to what that person tells you, and compare it with the message you started around the room. Odds are that what you hear will bear only the slightest resemblance to what you said.

Try it a dozen times, in a dozen different kinds of company. The result will almost always be the same. Because people don't listen.

"Oh, Lord, if I could only teach them to listen. How can they expect to find out what they need to know to make the sale, if they won't listen to the prospect?" You're hearing the complaint of a professional sales trainer with two decades of teaching and training experience.

Listen.

A woman just came through the door of your toy store, moving quickly. She didn't look around at all. Just located you, saw you were connected with the store, and headed right for you.

You greeted her. "Good morning. Can I help you?"

"I hope so. I can't imagine how it happened, but I forgot my grandson's birthday, which was yesterday. My daughter, son-in-law, and grandson are coming to visit us in about an hour, and if I don't have something to do with firemen for the child, he'll be heartbroken. You know how they are, get fixed on one thing and that's it. Next week, it will be policemen or soldiers. Can you help me?"

You look at her. Middle-aged, very simply dressed, probably doesn't want to spend too much.

"Oh, I'm sure we can. We're out of firehouse sets at the moment, but he'd be delighted with this Fort Apache set. It has lots of soldiers and Indians. Children really love it." You shift a little, start to move toward the Fort Apache set, a few feet to your right.

She doesn't move with you, looks toward the Fort Apache set, then starts to move, stops, looks indecisive. Suddenly wheels, starts out the door again. "Thanks, but no. I'll try somewhere else. Thanks anyway." She's out the door.

You're nonplussed. You follow her to the door, look outside, watch her cross the street and get into a double-parked Cadillac driven by a casually dressed middle-aged man, obviously her husband.

As you turn away from the window, your eye is caught by the great big fire engine you've been trying to unload since last Christmas.

Oh. She said, ". . . something to do with firemen." That was the key phrase. Her grandson may be interested in soldiers next week, but not now. It was a rush; you didn't give it your full attention and you didn't listen well enough. You still have the great big fire engine, and she's gone down the road to the department store in the shopping center, where she'll probably buy a great big fire engine.

Listen.

You were stumped. You'd shown the young couple riding with you six houses in the last two weekends, two of them meeting every specification they'd described in talking about the kind of house they wanted.

But somehow it hadn't jelled, and you couldn't figure out why. He had a good job; she was expecting their first child. They'd both grown up in the country, lived in a city apartment, wanted to move out into the near suburbs. That was your meat; you'd been selling to just that kind of client for years. Still do. And you'd shown them nice houses, well within their means. Houses to start in and grow from, but with much more space than the city apartment they now occupied. They kept looking, saying the houses were very nice, but somehow not quite what they had in mind. In a way, they seemed as puzzled as you, no longer seemed to know quite what they wanted. They kept having the same private, quiet conversation about how it was in the little town they'd both grown up in, about the school and the church and Mom's house and all that.

Oh, wait a minute.

"Excuse me, Mrs. Williams. I think I may have missed something. Would you mind describing your mother's house to me? I've been listening to you folks talk, and it sounds as if it was a lovely place to grow up in."

It had been. Mrs. Williams described a large, rambling country place on the main street of a very small town, and about midway in the process of doing so all three of you realized that the house they were looking for was the house she was describing, rather than the very nice, smallish "starter" houses you'd been showing. You wound up finding and selling them the house of their dreams, all right. It cost half again what they'd been prepared to pay. They somehow managed it, and live there to this day, with the child she was expecting and three more since then.

Listen. And learn to listen to what they're really saying.

QUESTIONING

Listen and question. If you're not sure of what you're hearing, ask. The answers to your questions will often tell you exactly what you need to know to make the sale.

Ask the kinds of questions that take you somewhere, such as:

- Who is it for?
- What kind of widget did you have in mind?
- When do you need it?
- Where do you intend to put it?
- How do you intend to use it?

These kinds of questions develop information, enable you to target the real needs and wants of your customer, in fact often cause the customer to better define those needs and wants. The very process of developing information therefore both enables you to sell most effectively to the customer and enables the customer to join you in the selling process.

Beware the "why" questions. They often take you nowhere useful, function to slow down the development of the selling situation. Thus "Why do you want it?" no matter how skillfully asked, moves the prospective buyer toward a reconsideration of the whole situation, rather than toward a reaffirmation of needs and wants.

Beware the question that calls for a "yes" or "no" answer. More on that kind of question when we get deeper into the selling process.

PUT YOURSELF IN THE OTHER GUY'S SHOES

Listen and question and put yourself in your customer's shoes.

It's called *empathy,* and as with most words, every good dictionary has several meanings covering different kinds of usages. That definition that best fits our use of it in selling is: "Understanding so intimate that the feeling, thoughts, and motives of one are readily comprehended by another."

What you do is to empathize with your customer, which is "to feel or experience empathy." It's the process of putting yourself in the other guy's shoes.

It's probably the most important and most misunderstood aspect of selling.

Many of those in the business of sales training maintain that "You can't really teach someone how to sell. You can sharpen their skills, develop sound product knowledge, but you can't show them how to really listen, learn, empathize." Others, notably the old-fashioned "They buy from me because they love me" kind of salesmen (see Willy Loman in *Death of a Salesman*), insist that all that matters is empathy. What's striking about both points of view is that they're both wrong, because they're incomplete. Successful selling is a mixture of putting yourself in the other guy's shoes, sound selling skills, and keen and constantly updated product knowledge. Neither Willy Loman nor the mechanically sound "skilled" modern salesman with seven (or is it seventeen?) alternate ways to close the sale is very good at it.

But the alert small business owner—highly motivated to succeed, proud of his or her place of business and knowing the business well, able to listen, question, and empathize—can become a very skilled sales professional indeed.

SEVEN

Why They Buy

Wants and Needs / Rational Covers for Irrational Acts

"WHY DO I ALWAYS HAVE A LINE AT THE GAS PUMPS? That's easy to answer. I sell the cheapest gas in town," says the owner of a discount gasoline business.

"They come here to see and be seen. And they pay the price gladly. Very frankly, I think that business improves every time we raise our prices. They love to talk about how much they've spent to dine in the *grand luxe* manner," says the manager of an extremely expensive restaurant.

"Higher prices? Sure, I charge a little more than some other places. But I give them quality and they know it. Besides, if they asked the clerks in the discount stores some of the questions they ask me, and took the answers seriously, an awful lot of rooms would get painted two or three times in the same year. When I tell them to use something, I tell them how and when to use it, too. They appreciate that," says the owner of a large paint store.

Why do people buy? In a very real sense, that's too general a question. That's the kind of broad question that gets you into the whole area of market research, with emphasis on motivation research. At best, you find yourself with some general reasons for buying, some discussion of "wants and needs," some rather oversimplified pop psychology on rational buying motives, irrational buying motives, some general ways of stimulating people

41

to buy. You're highly unlikely to find insights into why people buy *your* merchandise from *you,* at *your* place of business, *now.*

Why do *your* customers buy what *you* have to sell, *now?* That's the right question. And a related question—based on your analysis of why they buy what they buy, now—what else will they buy that you can stock and profitably sell?

The problem in analyzing buying motives lies largely in a too-general approach. It's always tempting to construct grand generalizations about "why they buy," rather than doing the hard, specific thinking necessary to figure out why they buy from *you, now,* and what else they'll buy in the future.

Correct and specific analysis of customer buying motives has proven crucial for the survival of many individual businesses and sometimes of whole groups of businesses.

An example is that of the family grocery store. Before the Second World War, the family grocery was one of the most common kinds of small businesses.

But after the war, with the move toward the suburbs, much wider use of the automobile, and the growth of the supermarket and shopping plaza, the family grocery began to die out. Today, it exists as a "convenience store." And even as a convenience store, with very long hours, family groceries have a hard time making ends meet.

Except for those who have gone one major step further, and combined delicatessen and fast-food sections with their established grocery businesses. Now, many former family groceries have added hot and cold sandwiches, take-out platters of all kinds; have gone into modest catering operations, supplying specialty foods and party supplies; have added such equipment as pizza ovens and steam tables. Many such operations are flourishing, profitable businesses. They continue to sell groceries, but as a smaller and smaller factor in gross business and net profits.

It often required planning and relocation to nearby areas of high traffic and visibility for these kinds of businesses to survive. Those who did not analyze, adjust, move, and change their thinking often simply went out of business.

As those grocers who survived found, one of the crucial first steps was to clearly see what their customers were buying and why. They tended to keep good records, were able to see that some of the traditional grocery items were being bought less and less, as the supermarket competition began to be felt. They saw that frozen foods, prepared foods of all kinds, ready-cooked meats all began to move ahead in sales relative to other goods they sold—and especially just before lunch and dinner and on weekends.

They began to sell some sandwiches. Simple enough. If you're selling bread, meat, and "the fixings," anyway, it's easy enough to put them together and sell a ready-made sandwich. What was startling, though, was how people were willing to pay much more for a ready-made sandwich than for the parts of the sandwich if bought separately. Even if you figured in the labor—which was not usually done, as the grocer was in the store anyway—profits on those ready-made sandwiches were huge compared to the profits on groceries.

And so it went. Once they had seen where the future was for them, alert grocers knew what they had to do to stay in business and prosper. Those who didn't know how to take the first analytical and action steps are now managing supermarkets for others or have retired.

WANTS AND NEEDS

The day that people start buying what they need, really need to survive, something over half the businesses in the United States will start making preparations to permanently close their doors.

Putting it a little differently, people buy what they want and what they need. Often, they buy items that satisfy both wants and needs.

A man's suit can easily cost $100, often much more. A man's winter overcoat can easily cost another $100. Men can clothe themselves more warmly and durably in "work" clothes, costing a total of $50 to $75. The need is for $50 worth of clothes; the want costs at least another $150.

The woman driving that Cadillac which just passed you paid at least $5,000 to satisfy the "want" part of her automobile purchase. She could have gotten the transportation she needed, just as durably and reliably, for a great deal less.

Hobbies, cosmetics, sports, movies are all "wants," not survival-need satisfactions. Utilities, some foods, and some clothing are examples of items that are largely "need"—though of course how high you keep your thermostat affects your need for home heating fuels.

Practically speaking, wants become needs. Most people buy what they think they need, and never realize that they are buying because they want, not because they need. Most often we sell not to real need but to that kind of "felt need."

Customers buy for all kinds of reasons that have nothing to do with needs—style, prestige, their own images of themselves, convenience, greed, fear, love are all examples of basically irrational "wants."

Experienced sellers know that and develop their selling appeals around wants, while stressing how their products satisfy the felt needs of their customers. They tend to speak of benefits in terms of the wanted things their products will do, rather than the real needs the products will satisfy.

The carpet you're selling "looks good, and will for a long time." You're not as likely to sell it if you tell your customer that the carpet "is very durable, because it's so well made. It will cover your floor adequately for a long time."

The dress you're selling "looks wonderful on you, and it's in the height of style." There are other important things to say about the dress that will help justify the buying decision, but how that dress looks on your customer and how it will look to others are your main selling appeals. Without looks and style, it's probably no sale.

"That car is the top of the line" usually means that the customer is going to be asked to pay considerably more for appearance and prestige than is justified by any real use differences between the top-of-the-line car and the next model down. The engines and other main working parts are quite likely to be substantially, sometimes exactly, the same. An astonishingly large number of customers do pay the higher price, gladly paying the differential for imagined "top-of-the-line" advantages, while in fact quite irrationally reaching for the more desired appearance and prestige associated with the purchase.

RATIONAL COVERS FOR IRRATIONAL ACTS

Buyers and sellers often, in a sense, collaborate in agreeing upon seemingly rational reasons for irrational purchasing acts.

It's not as strange as it sounds. There is potential guilt in many buying decisions, and the experienced seller knows that, empathizes, and tries to make the buying decision an easier one. A very common instance is in the purchase of a more expensive item because it "looks better." The classic case is that of the color-coordinated, expensive appliances in the American kitchen, many of which cost substantially more because of their size, color, style, and useless gadgetry.

But let the appliance seller try to talk some of those who buy those appliances into buying smaller, plainer, simpler appliances that cost less initially, are less expensive to run and less expensive to repair. It doesn't work. Many people have learned to want those big, costly, wasteful appliances, and have convinced themselves (not without help from manufacturers, suppliers, and retailers) that they are somehow "better." The appliance dealer soon learns to sell customers what they want to buy.

First Contact

W E'RE INTO THE HEART OF THE MATTER NOW.
We've discussed the main attitudes and understandings you must have when preparing to sell successfully:

- Pride in yourself and and your place of business.
- The ability to empathize with your customers and understand their needs.
- How to sell benefits, rather than product features.
- The need for broad, deep knowledge of your own product lines, to help customers get maximum benefits out of what you have to sell.
- What total communication means, and how to be constantly alert as to what you are really communicating.
- The importance of listening, hearing what the customer is telling you, and using the knowledge gained to make sales.

Now let's discuss what happens at the center of the selling process—you and the potential customer face to face.

SAM WARD'S CHAIR

On Saturday, Sam Ward looks like a bum.

He's not, really. Sam is a high-powered, highly paid corporate executive who puts on what he calls his "fancy working clothes"

47

every weekday morning, boards a commuter train, and heads for Chicago. On Saturdays, unless he's traveling on business, he puts on the kind of old clothes he wore as an Indiana farm boy during the Depression—he says they're the only things he really feels comfortable in—and drives a six-year-old station wagon around town.

Sam takes work home evenings and weekends and spends quite a few hours in his office at home, doing some of the things he never seems to have time for in the office. Which is why he's out looking for an office chair this bright sunny spring morning, prepared to pick one out, pay for it, put it in the back of his station wagon, and start using it this weekend. He'll go for a pretty good executive chair, something in the range of $200 to $300.

Sam studied the local telephone book over breakfast and found two stores specializing in office furniture in the area, one a few miles away and the other five miles further on.

After breakfast, he set out for the nearest store, considering it an auspicious beginning when he was able to park on a meter right in front of it. It was a good-looking, large, airy store, clearly had the kind of chair he was looking for. He went in.

It was still fairly early, and he seemed to be the only customer. The only other people in sight were two men, both well dressed, both apparently employees, sitting toward the back of the store. One had a cup of coffee in his hand and a lit cigarette in an ashtray on the table before him. The other was smoking a big cigar, had his coffee on the table. Neither paid any attention to him, though Sam thought they must have been aware he'd come in.

He waited, just inside the door. Nobody moved. After a minute or so, he slowly walked back toward them.

As he approached, the man with the cigar turned toward him, spoke with his cigar still in his mouth. "Anything I can do for you?" He was far from cordial, looked as if he'd been disturbed at breakfast.

Sam was equally short. "Maybe. I wanted to look at some office chairs."

It was a strong cigar. One of the things Sam liked least about his job was the occasional necessity of breakfast meetings with cigar-smoking colleagues. This cigar was as strong as any of those he'd objected to over the years.

The man puffed, took the cigar out of his mouth, gestured with it. "Office chairs are over there, by the desks. If you see anything you like, let me know." The conversation was over.

Sam shook his head sadly, once, turned, walked straight back to the front door, and was on his way to the second store within sixty seconds.

Fifteen minutes later he was at the other store. This one was considerably smaller, surely had some chairs, but seemed unlikely to have the kind of chair Sam had in mind.

Sam went in. There was one man in sight, toward the rear of the store, on his feet with a book in his hand, apparently checking stock. Well dressed, in his forties, probably the owner. The kind of volume he'd have on a Saturday morning would scarcely warrant bringing in much help.

He saw Sam come in, smiled, put his book down, moved to meet Sam. Sam stopped, let him come.

The other man stopped when he'd reached Sam, smiled in a very straightforward and friendly way, met Sam's eyes directly.

"Good morning. Can I help you?" His tone, manner, relaxed posture all conveyed ease and the sense that Sam was a guest in his home; that it was a real offer of help, not the start of a high-pressure sell.

"Perhaps you can. I'm looking for a good heavy office chair for my home office, something with a high back that I can sit and read in. Do you have something like that?"

"Yes, we do indeed. Let me show you what we have." He smiled again, started moving back toward the rear of the store. Sam followed, smiling to himself. The selling process had started, and very well.

Oh, yes, Sam Ward bought a chair that day, in that store. And an office table he'd been thinking about, too. He told George Weiss—who was, as he had thought, the proprietor of the store—the story of the cigar-smoking nonsalesman in the first store, and that George ought to send him a finder's fee, for setting up George's sale so well. George laughed, said he would, except that salesmen like that gave everybody in the business a bad name.

The kinds of attitudes Sam Ward encountered in the first furniture store he visited were strikingly bad. Unfortunately, those attitudes are not as unusual as they ought to be.

"The customer comes first."

"When you open your doors, you have to be ready for business."

"No smoking on the selling floor."

"Show, don't point."

"If you don't like people, you shouldn't be selling."

You can add your own favorite maxim. They all apply, and more. The two men in the first furniture store shouldn't have been having breakfast with the store open and the whole selling area unattended. In that early-morning situation, with the store empty and Sam obviously looking for help, one of them should have dropped everything, including the cigar or cigarette, and come forward to offer help, as George Weiss did in the second store. When asked for something specific—in this instance, office chairs—the seller should have gotten right to work, showing and selling the merchandise.

Above all, the attitude displayed was simply unfriendly. Sam Ward did exactly the right thing in leaving. There was no reason to waste time with those people.

Sometimes sellers forget that the customer can do that—just walk away. The truth is that the customer has the last word in every selling situation, can terminate any discussion by simply leaving.

George Weiss did it right. He watched Sam come in, saw he was looking for help, dropped everything and moved to meet him. He was easy, relaxed, friendly, clearly ready to offer genuine help. There was nothing faked or forced about his first contact, and it set the stage for a completely successful presentation and close, followed by an add-on sale. Like most topnotch professionals, in selling or anything else, George Weiss made it look easy and natural.

ATTITUDES AND ACTIONS

Your real attitudes show.

"But I'm only human. You can't expect me to have a sunny disposition, day in and day out. There are family problems, business problems, people come in and try to steal me blind, and besides my feet hurt toward the end of the day."

Of course. All true. But the fact remains—your real attitudes show. If you can't continue to meet your customers in a genuinely friendly, even-tempered way, then either find a different way of making your living or get someone else to do the selling. You can't fake attitudes. How you really feel about the people who come through your front door shows in many ways—in the set of your mouth, whether or not your body is relaxed, how you move, how you talk, how patient you are, what questions you ask, how well you listen. If you try to fake attitudes, people will come away with a vague feeling of uneasiness, a certain distaste, even when they can't quite pin down what's bothering them about you. And that vague feeling of distaste is often the difference between making or not making the sale.

That usually accounts for the phenomenon of the "sour" salesman, with years and years of experience, who inexplicably goes into a slump, can't close sales any more. The formal and technical skills are still there. The product knowledge is still there. But something's missing. The smile is a little forced. There's usually a tendency to sell too hard, not seeming to allow enough time and attention to develop empathy, to size up the customer's needs. Or a tendency to sell too softly, meaning that the will to sell successfully doesn't seem as strong as it used to.

But what has really changed is the genuineness of the salesman's response to the customer. Without genuine response, genuine friendliness, genuine empathy, none of the old "tried and true" moves work very well. The prospective customer recognizes a touch of falseness, is uncomfortable with it, and tends to leave the situation and the salesman. And the sale.

WHEN THEY COME THROUGH THE FRONT DOOR

Just what do you see when someone comes through your front door?

Try that question on a number of other small business owners and managers. Try it on those who work with you. You'll get answers ranging from "Someone I have to take care of," which is a very bad answer indeed, to "Someone I mean to meet, greet, and sell," which is a very good answer, but still a little short of the truth.

Think of it this way. Make an estimate of the amount you spend each year on simply keeping your doors open—rent, heat, light, telephone, minimum labor costs, your own time, and so on. Add to that what you spend on advertising and promotion, window displays, and the like. Get a rough total. Then estimate the number of people who come through your front door in the course of a year. Divide the costs by the number of people.

Perhaps you'll find yourself dividing $40,000 by 20,000 people. If so, in a way you have an investment of $2 in every single person who comes through your front door. Not an investment your accountant can put into your balance sheet—but certainly an investment.

Looking at it from that point of view, the main thing to bear in mind is that every single person who comes through that front door is a potential customer.

That means everybody, from the well-dressed middle-aged couple to the raggedly dressed teenager. And one sale leads to another. A dollar spent with you now may be a hundred dollars next week. Satisfied customers bring in more customers. Advertising and promotion may get you started, but word of mouth can make you or break you.

SMOKING, TALKING, AND INATTENTION

"Don't smoke. It may bother some of the customers, and it may smoke up the stock."

"Don't talk to each other too much. It makes the customers think you're not interested in them."

"Watch the customers, to see when to go over to them."

Sounds like a tough, old-fashioned boss talking to a couple of brand-new, scared kids on their first jobs, circa 1900, doesn't it? That's not America in the 1970's, is it?

Oh yes it is.

Not long ago, Harriet and Jim Wilson opened the store of their dreams—a boutique specializing in unusual and expensive clothes imported from all over the world. They had a very rough first few months, until someone pointed out that their store reeked with smoke. It was a little place, and they were both habitual smokers. Addicted as they were, they never realized what the place really smelled like to everyone coming in the front door.

Harriet and Jim lost a good deal of their early stock, too. It was smoke-impregnated, over a long enough period to make most of it a lost cause. Just as surely as if there had been smoke damage from a fire.

An extreme case, admittedly. In much less extreme cases, it happens repeatedly. Every day, people like Sam Ward are unnecessarily repelled by smoke, and people like Harriet and Jim turn others away without even knowing it.

Talking and inattention to customers are difficult problems. Aside from the attention that must be paid to other business, it's "only human" to start and then want to finish a conversation, even though a customer comes in right in the middle of it.

But that's not really the point. The main thing to consider is the question of timing—your timing. You need to watch your customers very closely, without seeming to do so, and determine in each instance when and how to make your first person-to-person contact.

It's also true that customers often don't want to interrupt you while you're finishing a conversation, but are nonetheless irritated at not being approached when they show that they want help.

TIMING FIRST CONTACT

Tom Michaels likes people. He genuinely likes others and likes selling to them.

"When someone comes into my place, I walk right up, smile my biggest smile, and say 'Good morning. I'm Tom Michaels. How can I help you today?' You'd be surprised at how many of them tell what they have in mind right then and there, and many sales flow from that simple greeting."

They sure do, Tom. But you'd be surprised at how many customers react badly to that aggressive-seeming approach, feeling rushed into a high-pressure selling situation when as far as they're concerned they've just come in to look around.

You can lose a lot of sales with a too-quick approach. Just as many as you can lose through inattention.

Of course, you're not going to commit the cardinal sin of letting someone come in and leave without being approached at all. That's just a waste, and one of the big advantages you have over a discount operation is precisely your ability to offer personal service.

You must watch. Let the customer come in, pause just inside the door, blink a couple of times to adjust to the normally darker indoors, begin to look around to see what areas of the store may have interest.

If the customer immediately begins looking for someone, as Sam Ward did, make an unhurried, open, friendly approach. If not—and most customers don't look for help immediately—wait. Look the customer over. Make sure the customer sees you, and knows where you are. See where the customer pauses, where there is casual interest, where there is real and very substantial interest, where there seems to be some puzzlement.

You needn't worry too much about when to approach if you develop the proper waiting-and-watching habits. The truth is that the best small business owners and managers develop what they think of as a "sixth sense" about when to make the approach. Of course, it isn't a sixth sense at all, but rather the fruit of years of good waiting-and-watching habits.

CONTACT

The first direct customer contact is often confused with how to greet a customer, which occurs a short but extremely significant time after the process of first direct contact is started.

First contact really starts at that moment you and the customer become aware that you are in direct contact and begin to move toward each other.

Sometimes it's Sam Ward and George Weiss, alone in George's furniture store. George saw Sam come in, smiled, put his book down. Contact, a small but significant time before they faced each other and spoke.

Sometimes it's contact across a crowded store or across a busy counter. The customer has looked around, suddenly straightens up and looks for help. You, with "eyes in the back of your head," right in the middle of helping someone else, take a split second to make eye contact, smile warmly, nod, and so indicate that you'll be over to help shortly. With that friendly first contact, the customer will wait, usually entirely satisfied to look around some more. Without it, the customer will feel unattended, ignored, perhaps walk out.

Contact continues when you move directly to the customer. Up until now, you've been sizing up the customer. Now, the customer is sizing you up.

Are you walking quickly, looking at several other things while moving toward the customer? It's quite usual to do so. The life of a small business owner is often hectic enough to encourage divided and scattered attention. But bear in mind that you're in contact with your customer while taking that walk, that the selling process has already started, and that the moves you make before you say a word to the customer may make or break the sale later on.

It is once again a question of attitude. Try to think of yourself as moving to greet someone you have invited into your home. Pay complete attention to the person you are moving toward. Move unhurriedly, even deliberately. Make and keep eye contact as you approach. Smile. You're meeting someone, and putting your best foot forward.

WHAT TO SAY

There's no single right greeting, no list of wrong greetings.

"Hi, what can I do for you today?" is wildly inappropriate in a restaurant specializing in haute cuisine, with everyone but the parking-lot attendant dressed in tie and tails. It may be just right from the combination short-order cook and counterman in the little diner you lunch in five days a week.

Actually, the question of what to say on first contact is considerably overstressed by those who do not understand that contact begins before you say anything.

If you can greet the customer by name, do. "Good morning, Mrs. Jones" tells her that you remember her, that she has a somewhat special place in your regard, is not a stranger who just came in off the street. On the other hand, beware of calling her Mrs. Jones if there is the slightest chance her name is Johnson. Using the wrong name is a small disaster.

Often, the simple "Good morning. Can I help you?" fits best into the kind of courteous, unpressured selling situation you want to develop, and is the logical next step in the process you started with eye contact and followed with a quiet, unhurried, full-attention approach.

Sometimes it's not a full approach, as in a situation in which you're waiting on someone else. Then it's a holding action—eye contact, smile, nod, a few words.

As long as your attitudes and nonverbal approaches are right, the first contact words themselves are not too important. Your words and attitudes should convey warm, courteous attention, and make it possible for the customer to respond with "Not right now, thanks. I'm just looking," or some similar deferral of the direct selling situation, without making the customer feel somehow pressured into a "fish or cut bait," "buy or leave" situation.

One first approach that is often used, but seldom well, is the "merchandise" approach. It consists of approaching a customer and going into a discussion of specific merchandise the customer is looking at, or of showing something to an approaching customer to gain attention, with "That's a very fine piece, isn't it?" or "We sell a lot of those; people are using them more and more these days" or "That's a lovely color, isn't it?"

Beware this technique. In the most skilled hands, used in a gentle, almost diffident way, it can work to make sales. But even then, in these days of consumerism and sales resistance, this is often viewed as nothing but prelude to a hard sell, with no real attempt to determine the customer's needs and respond to them helpfully.

NINE

Early Stages

*Well, I Was Thinking of Looking at Some Widgets /
Show and Tell and Question / More Than One Customer
at a Time / Special Care with Group Prospects*

E VEN AFTER CAREFUL, SKILLED FIRST APPROACHES, THE most common response to your words of greeting will be "No, thanks. I'm just looking."

Let them look. Say something like "Fine. Let me know if I can be of some help." Then move away; turn your attention to something else.

Don't press. Don't say "Fine. But is there anything in particular you're looking for?" That's pressure, or at least is often interpreted as pressure by the customer. Remember, we're all used to pressure selling tactics, and most of us have developed substantial resistance to anything that smacks of the hard sell. You can find ways to sell very hard and effectively indeed without the "hard sell."

The number of people who come into your place of business just to look around, with no thought of buying, is very small. When people come through that front door, they normally have buying something in mind. That's why such traditional "just looking around" places as bookstores actually encourage casual looking. Some bookstores, and very successful ones, encourage browsers with places to sit, even a perpetually brewing coffeepot for all comers. The experienced bookstore owner knows that the more browsers, the more sales.

Customers do want to look around, often come in with no more than a vague notion of what they might be interested in.

Or they may have several things in mind, want to look at all of them before focusing on any of them.

Sometimes they want to examine alternatives in terms of what they have or want to spend. Or to find out if what they're interested in is within their price range at all.

If, after some more looking, the customer has given no sign of wanting help, you have a decision to make. Will you risk a second approach, which if premature may drive the customer right back out the front door? Or will you let it go a little longer, continuing to watch and wait? Remember, once you've made first contact, you're in the selling situation. You and the customer are known to each other, and the customer will rarely leave, if you are close by, without telling you that nothing seemed suitable, or giving you some other reason for leaving. Therefore, when in considerable doubt about the wisdom of a second approach, wait. You're likely to get your opportunity to approach again before the customer leaves, in any case.

WELL, I WAS THINKING OF LOOKING AT SOME WIDGETS

Or dresses, lawn furniture, tools—any classification so wide that you don't know quite where to start. If you run a hardware store and someone wants to look at tools, or a boutique and someone wants to look at dresses, you're not very far from "I'm just looking."

At the point that someone expresses interest in your widgets, which may be in fact half the stock you carry, you may be tempted to ask several kinds of questions. After all, the next step is adroit questioning aimed at determining the customer's needs, isn't it?

The key word in the last sentence is "adroit." Some questions are excellent, some not too good, some terrible. And too many questions of any kind too soon are a poor idea.

Your probable reply to the customer's expressed interest in widgets will be something like "Good. We have quite a full line of widgets. If you'll step over here I'll show them to you."

Then go to the widgets. No more questions, until you're actually confronting row after row of widgets.

Then a further question. "As you can see, we have a large variety of widgets for all kinds of purposes. Perhaps I can be most helpful if you can tell me a little about how you intend to use the widget." All said very gently, almost casually, with good, direct eye contact.

The good early questions are the ones that help you understand the customer's wants and needs. Those questions tell you what you need to know to close the sale later, while building the customer's confidence in your genuine desire to be of help. Any question that can be answered with a straightforward "yes" or "no" is not very good, in that it may not take you toward the information you need to consummate the sale, and may even impede progress.

For example, you can ask someone looking at garden equipment a question like "Do you do a lot of gardening?" You may get a short, simple "No." If so, you've gotten nowhere and put a negative into your selling situation needlessly. Later on, when you're looking at a piece of equipment, your prospect may half-remember your question and not buy because the amount of gardening done doesn't seem to justify the expense.

Far better in the same situation to ask something like "What are you planting this year?" The answer to that question may lead you in the direction of the sale.

Another kind of not very good question is the one asked entirely out of sequence. There is always a temptation to try to close too soon. You tell yourself you're "just taking the prospect's temperature" and ask a question like "What do you think of this one?" But that's a real closing question, and a pretty clumsy one at that. Asked too soon, it can elicit a strong negative reaction.

Then there are the really terrible kinds of questions. Unfortunately, they are asked every day.

One of the worst early questions you can ask is any variant of "What did you want to spend?" If you're lucky, you get the most usual answer, which is "I'm not sure." Or perhaps a stated range so wide that it's almost the same as "I'm not sure."

But you may also get a fairly specific amount cited, which is way below anything you have to offer. And that's trouble, for from then on the sale is all uphill, when it didn't have to be at all. Many customers start with only the vaguest idea of what they want to spend, and are really inquiring as to both the kind of merchandise and its price.

Well, if you can't ask what the customer wants to spend, what do you show?

If you have a fair variety of prices, show something around midrange. You can always move up to higher quality and perhaps more functions performed; you can always move down to lower price for the same basic goods and functions. If you have only a couple of price choices, show the higher, generally, unless you have strong indications from the customer to the contrary. It's almost always easier to move down to a more acceptable price than to move up to a higher price.

Another kind of question is so bad that you're surprised when you hear it, astonished when you realize you've done it yourself. It's the question that insults the customer in some way.

Hold on, you may say. That just doesn't happen in my place of business.

Are you sure? Have you or anyone working for you ever asked a teenager a question like "You don't want to spend too much, do you?" That's the sort of question, even when asked with the best of intentions and in kindly fashion, that can ruin a sale as soon as it's out of your mouth. Nobody likes being a second-class citizen. Nobody likes the assumption that he or she has less to spend than anyone else who walks into your place of business. By the way, that teenager, perhaps raggedly dressed, may be carrying one of the family's American Express cards and be ready to spend as much as anyone else who walks in.

SHOW AND TELL AND QUESTION

In your own place of business, you're the seller. When you buy something you need elsewhere, you're the customer. Treat your customer as you would like to be treated yourself.

That means putting yourself in the customer's shoes, empathizing with the customer. You walk in, usually with some idea of what you want, size up the place, move toward where you think your general area of interest lies. After a little while, a seller approaches you, offers assistance. You accept help. You'll respond to a question or two, but aren't really able to respond to very many. If you could, you would have known what you wanted, found it, bought it, and been on your way.

Too many questions too soon confuse you, perhaps make you think the seller is trying to narrow your wants down to something the store has, that perhaps the store doesn't stock very much in your area of interest.

What you really want, now that you have a general idea of what you're interested in, is to see the stock. In the course of examining the stock, you'll get some idea of what the store carries, and will become able to respond to other questions, which will better define your wants and needs. You welcome that, will respond most favorably to a presentation when you know you've been exposed to the stock, have the alternative choices clearly in mind.

As a seller, then, you understand that the early moves in the selling process, after first contact and before presentation of the merchandise you're going to try to sell, are an essential part of the selling process.

The customer can shortcut some of the moves in the selling process. Sam Ward came in and told George Weiss what he wanted, saw what George had to offer, bought.

But you as a seller can't shortcut those moves without risking loss of the sale. If Sam Ward had come in and moved around a little, waved George off when he approached, finally said he was interested in looking at something that would help him to read more comfortably when he brought work home, George would have had to ask a good many questions as he showed Sam his merchandise. He would have wanted to know Sam's home reading and working arrangements, what the lighting was like, what kind of work Sam did. He would have been ready to show armchairs, swivel chairs, couches, lamps, desks, bookstands, and other desk accessories before he would have been able to focus on selling Sam a chair. It's quite possible that he might have sold

Sam something else that would have served Sam even better under those circumstances, too. But Sam knew what he wanted, and George sold him the chair.

MORE THAN ONE CUSTOMER AT A TIME

It's not at all unusual to spend a fairly quiet morning or even most of a day waiting for potential customers to come through your door, only to find that when they do come, they come several at a time. And somehow they manage to come when you don't have enough help to handle them, no matter how good a planner you are. Then you find yourself waiting on one and watching three others. You hope that you won't rush the sale you're trying to make and lose it, while worrying about one or more of the others leaving.

No one has ever come up with a very good way to handle that situation, but there are a few ways to minimize the risks involved.

The most important way of coping is to make contact, assure waiting customers that you know they are there, and that you will be with them as soon as possible. And without causing the customer you're selling to think you're trying to rush the sale to get to those waiting. A rushed selling attempt is often simply a lost sale.

There's nothing wrong with leaving a customer you're working with under certain conditions, though. Just don't do it often and don't make a habit of it.

If the customer you're working with says something like "Why don't you take care of someone else while I look around a little more?" or "Let me think about this for a minute while you take care of someone else," you're probably being told that the customer feels that the presence of others is exerting pressure to make a buying decision prematurely. Many people don't like to make a hurried decision, feel that they're holding up others while they're trying to make up their minds. Under those circumstances, the best thing to do is to smile and say something like "All right. Suppose I see if I can relieve the congestion here a little, and get right back to you." The implication is that you're not shifting your attention at all, but rather clearing away some distractions so that you can focus completely on the wants and needs of your current customer.

Or you may be in a situation, as with some articles of clothing, in which the customer is about to try something on. Then, making sure that your customer agrees, you can say something like "While you're trying that on, I'll see if I can relieve some of the congestion out here, if that's all right with you. If you have any questions or problems, just call me over." The customer will almost always assent to that suggestion, probably welcoming the chance to quietly consider the clothes being tried on.

But those are situations that require a great deal of care on your part. If you've gotten midway into a selling situation with a customer, in most cases you are best advised to finish the sale after reassuring the waiting potential customers. To break into the selling process often cools off the customer you've been working with and endangers the sale.

SPECIAL CARE WITH GROUP PROSPECTS

"I hate it when three people come in together. They ask three times as many questions, take up a lot of your time, and then when you think you have the real prospect sold one of the others destroys the sale."

"Me too. You never know who you're selling to. Sometimes you don't even know who to greet at the start. The husband's in one place, the wife in another, and she starts looking around for help. You go over and start talking. A minute later the husband comes over, and it turns out he's the buyer and doesn't get along with his wife."

"It's people with children that bother me. I can sell to a couple of adults all right, but when you go the whole route with someone, and she then turns to one of her children, who's been running around bothering everyone in the store, and the kid says no, she hates it because it looks uggy or icky, and screams and says she won't live with whatever it is I just thought I'd sold— well, that just drives me up the wall. It can spoil my whole day."

Those things do happen. There's no doubt that selling to a group is significantly different from selling to an individual.

But the key word is "different." Not necessarily that much harder. Just different.

In every group, the buying decision is going to be made primarily by a single person. Often in consultation, sometimes taking and sometimes rejecting proffered advice from other group members. That's true even in the closest-knit family groups. When a husband and wife seem to be making the closest kind of joint decision, they are almost always in truth ceding the decision to one or the other, with full willingness to go along from the one not really making the decision.

One of the most significant differences between group and individual sales lies in what you do before you even make first contact.

When an individual comes in, you carefully watch, size up the individual as best you can, try to see what the individual seems most interested in, figure out when to make first contact.

When a group comes in, you are interested in all those things, too. But additionally, and more importantly, from the first moment you see the group you are trying to assess who it is you will ultimately be selling to, who is the key selling focus in the group.

You'll get clues from the way the people in the group behave. True, if they divide up and look at several things at once in different parts of the store, you may be dealing with several kinds of main interests and several different primary buyers. Then you treat the situation as if you're dealing with several individual sales, and take them one at a time. But if they stay together as a group, there are some fairly usual signs to look for.

For example, a couple comes in. They stay together for a few moments. Then she stops and carefully examines some merchandise, while he casually looks, then wanders around a bit, not really seeming to get involved with any other merchandise. If that pattern continues, she's clearly there to buy, he to advise, agree, or even merely accompany.

Or the same couple comes in. He wanders around a bit while she focuses on some merchandise. Then she says something like "This might be just the thing," and he responds "No, I think something I saw over there might save me quite a bit of work.'' You're not quite sure, but he's probably the ultimate buyer, with you needing to present the product and make the sale to both of them at the start, ready to move it to either one as the situation develops.

The main thing is to watch groups closely, to try to assess as well as possible what the interactions are between the members of the group, to regard the group not as two or more individuals but as a buying unit containing a key buying person and one or more other parts. Your aim is to find the buying person, sell that person, and get agreement from the others in the group.

Approaching a group is a little different, too. Ideally, you want to approach the group while it's together and say something like "Good morning. Can I help you?" to whoever you think is the key person, while encompassing all the group's members in the greeting. If that's not possible, then your greeting should be directed toward the one you regard as the key person.

Don't be afraid to wait too long before approaching. Every bit of time you can spend observing the group can help in consummating the eventual sale. And groups are less likely to walk out than individuals. One or more of the group's members is likely to look for help before long.

Your early questions to the group can be very helpful in determining both the nature of their interest and whether or not you have correctly identified the key buying person.

If you ask a question like "How will this mainly be used?" or "Will one of you be using this more than the other?" you will soon be able to determine who it is you're really selling to—except in those increasingly rarer instances in which, no matter what is being bought, the husband regards himself as the real buyer, as controller of the family finances. That still happens, but not very often.

Beware the temptation to play off group members against each other. It looks easy, and once in a while may even work to make a sale. But even if it does work, it's likely to be the only sale you ever make to any member of that group. That's especially true when husband and wife are involved. Even if they buy after you've used the leverage caused by their disagreements, they are very likely to carry away a strong feeling that they've both been attacked, and not want to come back.

TEN

Show and Sell

*Presenting Benefits / Handling the Goods / Presentation /
Other People Seem to Like It Very Much / Price /
Deferring Other Early Objections / How to Handle
Competition / Planning Your Presentations / Presenting
to a Group / Taking Their Temperature*

T HE ACTUAL PRESENTATION OF YOUR MERCHANDISE EX-
tends naturally from the early stages of the selling process.
In fact, it is essential to understand that when in the early
stages you say "Yes, they're over here. Let me show you . . . ,"
you are at precisely that point hoping to ask the right questions,
get the right information from the customer, move into the
presentation, and make the sale.

That's important. You are not showing, then later on presenting and selling. You're showing and selling.

PRESENTING BENEFITS

The single best indication that you have successfully developed
information as to the customer's wants and needs comes when
you are able to say "I think this one will do exactly what you
have in mind" and have the customer reply, after you've presented the product, "You know, I think you're right. That
probably will do it."

For the focus is on what the product will do for the customer,
and, if at all possible, in terms of what the customer has told you
of needs and wants.

Putting it differently, it is never sufficient to demonstrate how good a product is; you must demonstrate how good it is for the particular customer you're selling to.

HANDLING THE GOODS

Have you ever seen a salesclerk pick up a piece of merchandise, wipe or blow the dust off it, and then try to sell it? Not often? No, and not successfully either.

Every piece of display merchandise in your place of business must be ready for demonstration and sale every minute your doors are open. That's one of the oldest axioms in the business world. An article unready for sale is often a lost sale.

When you or anyone working with you takes out, picks up, shows, demonstrates, presents any piece of merchandise that is for sale, it should be done gently and respectfully.

Present plumbing fixtures gently? Sell rugged outdoor goods gently?

Yes. Certainly. It's done successfully on television and in the newspapers every day.

Remember, people buy because they need, but even more because they want. And wanting is an emotional thing. They respond when you determine their practical needs and sell benefits in terms of those needs. But they also respond when they like what they see, feel, taste, smell, hear. And if you have chosen merchandise you feel is worth selling, and are offering it to them, offer it gently and respectfully. Show them you value it; they will value it all the more.

Don't make the very common mistake of trying to dramatically demonstrate the excellent qualities of your merchandise by abusing that merchandise. You can certainly prove that the jacket you're selling is hardy by pulling, squeezing, and trying to tear it as if it were a telephone book, but all you'll accomplish is to create the impression that you somehow are selling damaged goods and don't think much of those goods yourself.

One stationer recently reported that he had been demonstrating the hardiness of a line of looseleaf binders he carried by literally throwing them against a wall during sales demonstrations. When pressed, he admitted his sales hadn't gone up, but he was sure he'd made a considerable impression on many of his customers with that sales technique. He probably did, but not the impression he wanted to make. The binders were strong, all right. They were also attractively designed and had a nice, soft finish. What the stationer had succeeded in doing was to accentuate the practical benefits of hardiness and long life to the detriment of the emotionally satisfying benefits of beauty and touch. And at the same time, he had handled goods he had chosen himself violently, carelessly, damagingly, making those goods seem of very little value to him. It's a classic error.

Handle the goods carefully. For example, if you're demonstrating a machine, make very sure you know how to start and use that machine. There's nothing quite so chilling in that kind of selling situation as a machine that won't start. The used car salesman whose second-hand cars won't start has been a figure of fun ever since cars have been sold secondhand.

In fact, that kind of demonstration is one of the few instances in which it's perfectly all right to call in someone else. If you need help to demonstrate properly, it's far better to have it right at the start, rather than after you've run into problems.

PRESENTATION

At the point of presentation, there are many ways the selling situation can go. You may find that you have a quick and easy sale. More often, you'll find wants, needs, and reservations surfacing that haven't been apparent before, no matter how adroitly you've questioned and developed information. The whole sale may turn on something you had no inkling of when you started the presentation.

That's why in presenting you go right into the needs and wants you think the customer has indicated, and at the same time try to paint the whole picture in terms of all the main benefits to be gotten from the product.

It's a serious error to immediately focus sharply on perceived wants and needs to the exclusion of some of the other main benefits of the product.

For example, another stationer, perhaps a more skilled and experienced seller, might have presented the looseleaf binders differently. After learning that the customer was interested in a sturdy binder, he might have shown the same very sturdy binder, described how it was made to validate the claim of sturdiness, told a "proof" story about the binder to further validate the claim.

He might also have handled the binder gently and carefully, pointed out how well designed and therefore how easy to use it was; how well cover material and color went together, and therefore how well it would look on the customer's desk or shelf. It might have turned out that sturdiness was the stated main desire but appearance was even more important, something you cannot always know before going into the presentation.

The example is illuminating from another point of view. Very often, a prospect will start by giving you a rational reason for wanting a particular product or kind of product. And it's a real reason, one that must be satisfied by the seller or no sale will be made. At the same time, the seller finds that the sale seems ultimately to turn on quite another matter, such as appearance, what others will think of it, or cost, in the sense that sometimes "expensive" is equated with "good" or "prestigious." Then you must sell the emotional needs hardest and close the sale on those needs, while not neglecting to satisfy the practical need which was first stated.

Some say, "Sell the sizzle, not the steak," meaning sell the sense-satisfying emotional needs, not the practical needs. That may be all right for some impulse buys, but not for most of the goods small business owners have to sell. The right way is to know your steak very well, find out what needs that steak really satisfies for the customer you're selling, as well as the "sizzles" that appeal, and "Sell both the sizzle and the steak."

OTHER PEOPLE SEEM TO LIKE IT VERY MUCH

There are a lot of ways to put "testimonials," sometimes called "third-party material," into your presentations. And such material can be very useful in making sales, if used sparingly and at the right times.

Sometimes they are very general statements, like "We're selling a lot of these this year," or "We're having a hard time keeping these in stock," or "Here's a very popular model."

Sometimes they are "proof stories." "A man named Warren came in here day before yesterday and bought two of those. He came back yesterday afternoon about three o'clock for two more. Said his wife got hold of one and his daughter the other, and now he had to get one for his other daughter and still wanted one for himself. Looks as if I'd better order some more in a hurry." Watch out for this kind of story, unless it's true. People often have good noses for the exaggerating seller. And if your credibility goes, so does the sale. Be sure to make the story very specific and at least moderately checkable, if anybody wanted to take the trouble to do so.

Occasionally, you will use one or more letters from satisfied customers as testimonials. More likely than not, you'll have them available, quote from them, show them as seems desirable.

PRICE

People have a disconcerting habit of interrupting right in the middle of a presentation and saying: "Is this the best price you can give me?" "Do you have anything less expensive?" "If I buy three of them, do I get a discount?"

A very early price objection can cut off your presentation prematurely, force the whole selling situation to turn on the question of price rather than on customer benefits, and thereby ruin the sale.

That's what can happen if you respond directly to the objection. On the other hand, if you don't respond directly to an early price objection, the customer may see your lack of real response as an evasive attitude, and the sale may be ruined from the credibility direction.

Defer the price question or objection if you can, but with extreme care not to appear evasive. Be as direct as possible. Say something like "I'd like to show you what this can do for you. Perhaps we can hold the question of price for just a moment, until you have a full view of what you're buying." It usually works. The customer feels that you may be willing to talk about price without getting any kind of promise from you, while at the same time often recognizing the sense in what you're saying about getting the full picture. You have also used the early price question or objection as an opportunity to assume later sale of the product, and may be able to use the later price discussion as a means of closing the sale.

Don't respond to an early "Do you have anything less expensive?" question by immediately pulling out other less expensive items in your stock, unless of course you haven't even yet begun to present and are just beginning to show your merchandise to the customer. It's far better, once you are well started on your presentation, to finish—better for both you and the customer. Better for you in terms of moving the sale forward, with the customer forgetting the early price objections in the course of developing enthusiasm for the product you're presenting; better for the customer in that jumping around from product to product, never getting the whole picture of benefits on any single one, results only in confusion and an uninformed purchasing decision.

DEFERRING OTHER EARLY OBJECTIONS

That really is true of almost all the early objections. They are best deferred if possible. If they continue to be real questions in the customer's mind, you can be sure that they'll come up later on during the selling process.

Often the early objection is answered during the course of the presentation itself. The customer may say "That machine doesn't look very sturdy. Are you sure it will stand up under heavy use?" You may respond with "Yes, that's an important question. I think you'll see just how sturdy it is as we move along here." You know the question comes up all the time, already know how you're going to handle it, want to say a few other things first. Or you may be able to change the order of your comments a bit, and handle the objection as a question smoothly, in the course of your presentation.

You get a lot of insight into the weight and importance of the customer's early objection by simply listening. When the customer says something, stop talking, no matter how important you think your comments may be at that moment. Listen hard, paying full attention to what the customer is saying. If the question is make or break to the customer, you may have to handle it immediately. Or it may be something you can close with later.

Never say anything like "Yes. I'll get to that in a minute. Just let me finish what I'm saying about this aspect of it." That's an excellent way of losing the customer's attention, perhaps of destroying the sale. In industrial selling, where the "canned" or fully memorized presentation is still often used, the novice often proudly presents the longish memorized presentation, blithely moves past half a dozen pieces of information supplied by the buyer which should act as tools for developing interest now and closing the sale later, doesn't make the sale, and can't figure out what went wrong.

HOW TO HANDLE COMPETITION

Today, describing something as a "unique selling proposition" conjures up the image of the old-fashioned salesman lurking in the doorway of his store, hook in hand, waiting for some unsuspecting farm boy to come along.

It's a funny old phrase. Yet it describes an approach that is central to successful selling.

It goes considerably beyond "Don't knock your competition." When you are showing and presenting your product to a customer, as far as you're concerned the competition doesn't even exist. The customer has indicated certain interests, needs, wants. You have responded with merchandise which you believe will satisfy those needs and wants. That's all there is. You don't mention competitive products and businesses, and by so doing raise alternatives that may not even have occurred to the customer.

It really doesn't make much sense to say, during the course of a presentation, "You know, we think this is the best line of lawn mowers made. I know the store across the street still carries the Mills line, but we gave it up. Too many service problems. I know they've been having a lot of service problems, too."

The Mills line of lawn mowers? The store across the street? Didn't think of going in there, and perhaps I should before making a buying decision. Service problems? Oh, I hadn't thought of service problems with new lawn mowers. Maybe the old mower isn't so bad after all. It isn't as if it has broken down—maybe I'll have more problems with a new mower than if I just keep the old one. And what could have been a sale turns into a waste of time for all concerned.

Don't play "dirty pool" as regards your competitors. "I hear Joe Smith is going out of business. If you buy a car over there, you'll have to go thirty miles to have it serviced under warranty." That's dirty pool. Don't do it, and don't let anyone working with you do it, even if what's being said is true. It's bound to hurt your reputation and business standing in the community. And your own pride, which is one of your most substantial business and personal assets.

PLANNING YOUR PRESENTATIONS

When you have something to sell, and go through the process of selling it to a number of people, you develop a presentation. You may not necessarily think of it that way, or really intend to do so, but it happens. You find yourself describing the product in basically the same way to most prospective purchasers—starting with the same main features and benefits, stressing those key benefits that seem to apply to whoever you're selling, developing a body of proof stories and materials to help convince prospects of the truth of what you're saying and the quality of the product.

That might seem to be good enough. You listen to your customers, stay responsive to their needs, tailor your approach to those needs without neglecting in the main features of the product, make enough sales.

Or do you make enough sales? Is it possible that what really happens is that you fall into a presentation developed in the course of going through the selling process with your first few prospects, and in so doing fail to see some of the main potential uses of some of your products, and sell much less effectively than you might, as a result?

You can plan a presentation around each of the main products or product lines you sell. A presentation with a beginning, a middle, and an end that moves into closing the sale. A presentation that starts with your responses to the needs and wants information you've developed from talking with the customer, that goes on to discuss the main features and benefits of the product for that customer, within a discussion of all the main features and benefits of the product.

You are unlikely to use fully memorized presentations, though sometimes an almost-memorized presentation develops in the course of selling the same product hundreds of times. Most small business owners simply have too many products to sell to attempt to keep multiple presentations in their heads.

You can and should, however, think through an outline presentation on each main product or line you carry. In many instances, manufacturers' and distributors' brochures and other sales materials can be extremely helpful. After all, printed sales material attempts to present products in the most favorable light, and many of the professionals who develop promotional material know about the necessity of selling benefits, too. They don't have the enormous selling advantage of being able to tailor their presentations to individual customers, as you do, and so their material is often fairly general in nature, and needs to be adapted for your customers. But promotional material is often exactly what you need to form a basis for your own presentations—a track to run on, from which you can generate successful selling presentations.

Any new presentation you try will need refining as you go. You'll learn what appeals work for large numbers of your customers. You'll learn some product uses from your customers that neither you nor the promotional materials writer thought of.

As you use your presentation, you'll gather proof materials from satisfied customers. Many liquor store owners who make a real success of selling wine ask their customers to tell them what they think of new wines they are stocking and selling, then use satisfied customers' reports as proof materials.

Some very successful small business owners make a practice of making notes as soon as possible after a sale has been completed. They write down needs and wants that were satisfied, what appeals worked, what key objections were raised and handled, what words and phrases really seemed to hit home, who they sold to, what the situation was for proof-story purposes, and what add-on sales, if any, were achieved. It's worth doing.

PRESENTING TO A GROUP

The main estimate, for better or worse, has usually been made by the time you're really presenting to a group. You've probably by then made the best educated guess you could as to the key person in the group, and are presenting to that person.

It's important to watch the group carefully as you present. If you've made an error as to who the key person is, it's often possible to switch focus in midstream, concentrate on someone else.

While you're presenting to the key person, you will continually make and remake eye contact with the other members of the group, try to assess how your presentation is being received by each group member and by the group as a whole.

It's worthwhile to hesitate a little before taking up an early objection from one of the group members, to slow up your normal response pattern slightly. You'll be able to watch the group more easily, while giving other group members a chance to answer the early objections themselves. Often, group members will answer objections without waiting for you, and in so doing reinforce their own positive feelings about what you're selling by "getting into the act." No need to get into a family argument in this situation. Let the group members have their own disagreements, while you patiently wait your opportunity to get back on the presentation track. Remember—the disagreements people in a family or other group are having may go far deeper than a seemingly small disagreement about your product, and you get into their disagreements with considerable risk to the whole sale.

TAKING THEIR TEMPERATURE

The bane of a seller's life is the prospect who listens to the whole presentation, nods now and then, seems to agree that the product is the greatest thing since sliced bread, then doesn't buy and won't say why. A widely encountered variation is the prospect who listens, seems to agree, then asks a question or raises an elementary objection that seems to indicate the prospect never heard a word you said.

"Take the temperature" of your prospect periodically while presenting your product. See if the prospect is warming to what you're selling. If not, go back, ask questions, probe for areas of interest. Ask rhetorical questions such as "That's a pretty unusual feature, isn't it, Mr. Smith?"

Get agreement. "I think you'll agree that any full-sized car that gets almost 25 miles a gallon these days is worth taking a very careful look at, Mrs. Jones." You're looking for some kind of affirmative response—even a nod will do.

Sometimes it's called "trial closing," though the technique has little to do with closing the sale. Don't be misled by the "trial closing" tag; a little agreement during a presentation is hardly ever a signal to try to seriously close the sale. On the other hand, getting a little agreement during the presentation can be very helpful when you do start closing.

ELEVEN

Moving from Presentation Toward Sale

Don't Argue or Lose Your Temper / Seeing Hurdles as Opportunities / Anticipating Objections / Handling Hurdles / Listening to the Customer Object / Indicating Agreement with the Customer / Questioning to Clarify the Objection / Handling Customer Questions / Price Objections / Other Honest Objections / Convince Me More / Smokescreens / Obvious Evasions

"**Y**OU CAN'T SELL THEM ALL."

True. But that's also the usual song sung by unsuccessful, disheartened, often unskilled practitioners of the selling trade.

"You can sell a lot more of them than you think" is the response of the skilled, highly motivated sales professional.

For many sales professionals, the most interesting, challenging, stimulating part of the selling process starts when, with the product basically presented, the prospective purchaser indicates one or more specific reservations, questions, or specific objections; voices general reasons for saying "no"; or tries to avoid making a buying decision.

These kinds of reactions are often all lumped together and described as "objections." That is not a correct way to describe them all, as there are a wider range of motives than that. Sometimes they are described generally as "sales resistance," which is closer, but still not wide enough, as it does not, for example, properly describe those very straightforward questions on product use which can be the most valuable contributions the customer makes toward closing the sale.

We prefer to think of them as "hurdles," by which we mean any and all things the customer may come up with that are real or potential threats to your closing the sale now.

And, as every seller knows, there are a lot of them.

DON'T ARGUE OR LOSE YOUR TEMPER

Whatever reaction the customer has, there is surely one reaction you as seller may not have. You simply can't afford to lose your patience, your temper, or in any way convey even the slightest sense of argumentiveness to the customer. There's no surer way to lose the sale.

In many selling situations, there are ample reasons to argue, to be impatient. For example, you've just made a full and seemingly well-received presentation, taken the customer's temperature several times with favorable results, and at the end asked what the customer thought of the product. You may even be thinking that this will be one of those rare situations in which the customer will say "Okay, when can I get delivery?" Then you'll unhurriedly take out the order book and write up the sale. Except that the customer responds with "No, I'm not buying today, just looking. Anyway, I think I can get something just as good across the street for half the money."

Or the customer starts asking questions which make it perfectly clear that not a word of your presentation got through.

Or the customer consults a watch and says "Oh, I didn't realize how late it was. Thanks very much; it was very interesting."

Perhaps it's one of the hundred variations of "You salespeople are all alike. I don't believe a word of it."

It doesn't really matter what it is that can set you off—the main thing is, don't let it.

It may help to understand that the reaction you're seeing may not be the customer's real reaction, but a cover for backing away from the selling situation. Like the rest of us in many business and personal situations, the reaction is often on an unconscious rather than a conscious level.

Nor are most customers "slow" or "stupid," as the impatient seller sometimes assumes. You are selling out of a completely familiar environment, where you literally know every square foot of the terrain. You should; you spend much of your waking time there. The customer, in an unfamiliar place, trying to adjust, is easily distracted by unfamiliar lights and objects.

And you are showing and selling completely familiar products; you may even have gone too quickly because of that familiarity. The customer is seeing everything for the first time. It can take quite a while to absorb a new product in a new place.

There's one other factor well worth considering. That's the world we all live in. It's a world full of products, slogans, and advertising claims—a world of "hype" and the "hard sell." No wonder customers tend to look upon you initially with a certain skepticism, no matter how effectively you make first contact, move to and through the presentation. Unfortunately, hardly anyone trusts anyone else out there selling. Bear that particularly in mind at precisely the moment you begin to respond with "No, that's not true," "I don't think you're right about that," or even the classic lost-temper response: "Look, are you calling me a liar?"

SEEING HURDLES AS OPPORTUNITIES

The customer who "rolls over and plays dead" after your undeniably superb presentation is a pretty rare bird. Much more often, the presentation gets all kinds of other responses from the customer, all the way from "Sorry, I'm just looking today," to "I wouldn't be caught dead with that thing in my house."

The toughest hurdle of all, though, is no reaction at all—the customer who lets you present, listens, then says "No. I'm just not interested." There's no way to the sale from there, unless you can shake that reaction.

That's the basic reason why sales professionals regard seeming hurdles as very real opportunities to sell. Once the customer gives you a reason for not buying—any reason—you at least have some dialogue going, some way to respond, persuade, probe for wants and needs. It's the same in most person-to-person situations: once you start talking, barriers seem to melt away.

ANTICIPATING OBJECTIONS

A solid, complete product presentation often goes a long way toward short-circuiting many of the most common hurdles you face in making the sale. When you've shown a customer just how well your product is made, observed that the manufacturer thinks so much of it that it's guaranteed for a full year for both parts and labor, and then driven home the long-life and minimum-care benefits of the product, the customer isn't likely to say "But it doesn't look as if it will last." And if the customer does, it's an opportunity to strongly present those features and benefits again and turn the objection into an opportunity to close the sale.

Sometimes manufacturers and distributors will supply material that enables you to anticipate common objections and work answers into your presentations. Equally often, you will start to sell a product, go through the first few presentations "learning the ropes"—which to a large extent means learning from customer responses—and then develop your own set of previous answers to anticipated objections.

There is one main hazard to be avoided—that you will work into your presentation answers to objections that may never come into your customers' minds. That hazard is most easily and permanently handled by being sure that you deal with anticipated objections always in terms of the positive features and benefits of your products.

For example, you might, if selling FM radios, point out the "excellent fringe-area reception of this model. People tell us that with this exclusive channel lock-in feature, they get their favorite stations loud and clear, from as far as 75 miles away."

You would not say "People around here have been having trouble with their FM reception for a long time. They tell us that with this model, featuring the channel lock-in device, they get stations 75 miles away, loud and clear."

You might say "This radio is sturdily built, and at the same time very light and compact. It's all done with miniaturization and shock-resistant plastic."

You wouldn't say "This radio looks a lot more fragile than it really is. Looks as if it wouldn't take much to flatten it, doesn't it? But appearances are misleading: they do so much with miniaturization and shock-resistant plastic these days.''

The customer may have no idea that FM reception in the area is a problem, may never have thought that the radio is anything other than light and sturdy—it's guaranteed, isn't it? On the other hand, if those objections are common ones, they may be best handled before they can be raised, in so positive a way that they can be turned into good reasons for buying.

HANDLING HURDLES

When your customer has something to say, stop talking and start listening. Always remember that:

- Your customer may want to say something that may lead you right to the sale.
- You'll get a chance to properly present the product, if that's the best road to the sale—but the object of the whole exercise is to make the sale, not to "present" the product.
- Your customer can terminate the conversation at any time, by turning and leaving.

The first step in handling hurdles, then, is to listen to the customer, attentively and in a relaxed fashion.

LISTENING TO THE CUSTOMER OBJECT

Use the time spent listening to the objection or question to observe the customer, to try to assess the customer's attitudes toward the product, the place, you, the buying decision.

Show that you're listening. Let your interest in what the customer is saying show in the way you nod your head. Don't worry that nodding will seem to give the wrong impression that you're agreeing with the objection—it will be taken as attention. Emphasize that you're listening in a friendly way with a smile. Caution here—there are friendly smiles and there are wise-guy smart-alecky smiles, and you'll turn your customer away if your smile is misinterpreted.

If you're an arm-folder, break the habit. If you want to see just about the worst thing you can do while listening to someone else, just fold your arms and smile, even your warmest, friendliest smile.

INDICATING AGREEMENT WITH THE CUSTOMER

While listening, indicate with face and manner that the customer is making a reasonable comment. Your whole attitude will defuse possible confrontation. You're not out to win an argument, but to make a sale.

When you respond verbally, you will almost always say something like "That's a reasonable question," "I can see your point of view," or "I can understand that."

Even when your response adds up to "Yes, but . . . ," you will want to use a longer phrase, to dignify the customer's point of view or question, and not seem to dismiss it out of hand.

QUESTIONING TO CLARIFY THE OBJECTION

Quite often, you'll want to ask the customer questions before directly responding to a question or objection.

It may be as simple as not quite understanding what the customer said or meant, in direct question-and-answer terms.

Or you may size up the situation as one calling upon you to smoke out the customer's real question or objection. Then you will want to do some probing.

Whatever your reason, don't be afraid to answer a question with a question, as long as you're not doing it as a form of argument. But be careful not to do it too often or in a series of questions piled atop questions. It's funny when Abbott and Costello do it; it can be infuriating to a customer and destroy the selling situation.

HANDLING CUSTOMER QUESTIONS

When a customer asks a question that can be answered in a straightforward and factual way, do so.

But don't let it stop there. The customer who asks you a factual question on a matter that you had already discussed in your presentation is signaling that a partial re-presentation may be desirable, that perhaps you didn't get through on some points the first time around. By all means, re-present the main positive features and benefits of the product, stress the desirability of the product, and try to close the sale around the re-presentation. You may feel that the seemingly straightforward factual question is really a way of registering a hidden objection, or of providing a basis for backing away from the buying decision altogether. In either of those cases, you will probably elect to answer the question as asked, while at the same time trying to uncover and handle the real objection so that you can move toward the sale. You can do that with re-presentation and an attempt to close the sale, and with probing questions of your own.

PRICE OBJECTIONS

These are prudent times. Yesterday's big spender is often today's worrier. Fuel is short, prices are high, educating your children is an enormous cost. Buying a house involves numbers with more digits than they ought to have. Inflation and unemployment won't go away.

Still, when someone says "It's too expensive," "I can't spend that much," "Do you have anything for less?" or "Maybe I can get it for less somewhere else, " you can't be sure it's price that's being objected to. It may be that want and need haven't been firmly enough established, or that other objections haven't been satisfactorily answered.

On the other hand, when someone says "No, I'm just looking," "I'll think about it," or "I'm not convinced this is for me," you may really be hearing a price objection.

There's very little real question about it—price today is the toughest single objection you face. And it's getting tougher.

There are no easy answers. Many of the products small businesses sell can be gotten a little cheaper at discount stores, can be put off, can be "thought about a little more." The only real answers for small business owners are in the areas of quality, service, convenience, reliability—and selling skills.

Sometimes, you will hear a "too high a price" objection; sometimes a "not enough money" objection. You'll probably do exactly the same whichever objection you may later decide you heard. You'll keep on trying to sell what you've been trying to sell so far, until you've either made the sale or felt forced to show and sell something less expensive that may still satisfy enough wants and needs to make your customer want to buy.

The worst mistake you can make in a price objection situation is to go down in price or to different merchandise too soon. It's almost always desirable to re-present, to search for ways to accentuate benefits in terms of needs indicated, to find ways of stretching out payment if the customer seems a good credit risk. You can't know until you've tried hard to sell again whether you're running into a real unwillingness or inability to spend the money or into some other unstated objections.

Early on in the selling situation, you of course have a great deal more leeway. If you show something medium-priced and immediately run into substantial and, as far as you can tell, real price resistance, by all means drop down to less expensive merchandise. Later, after going through the presentation of the merchandise, you can't drop down so easily. If you do, you run the very substantial risk of having sold the more expensive merchandise so well that the less expensive, and usually necessarily less attractive, merchandise is no longer acceptable to the customer. Then you lose the sale from either direction. The more expensive merchandise costs too much; the less expensive isn't good enough.

If you decide you must go down, go to different merchandise rather than cutting prices on the merchandise originally offered. The small business has a seeming advantage over the larger one, in its seeming ability to develop more price flexibility, but that flexibility is often a trap. Once the word gets around that you can be "beaten down" on price, you're in trouble. Then you're in the unenviable position of having a full service business with full service costs and a cut-rate price structure. That's a sure recipe for bankruptcy.

OTHER HONEST OBJECTIONS

There are dozens of simple, honest reasons for not buying what you have to sell. When you encounter one, you have no choice but to deal with it, overcome it, and use the leverage gained in overcoming it to move ahead to closing the sale.

A large group of objections can be thought of as product objections. They will range all the way from not liking the variety of colors offered to not thinking the product will do the job you claim it will do.

Product objections are best answered out of your own product knowledge, by redemonstrating specific features questioned, and by proof stories. The best possible answer to "It looks too fragile" is to show again just how sturdy the product is, talk about its guarantees, use proof stories.

There are also objections that have nothing to do with you, your place of business, or the specific product you're trying to sell. Sometimes people develop brand preferences, mistrust the service policies of certain manufacturers, want to be reassured that the buying decision now will not cause them a good deal of bother later.

Those kinds of objections are best met by your personal reassurance that you stand behind what you sell—that you wouldn't be selling the product if you didn't have confidence in it and its manufacturer or distributor. Caution—if you say you're behind something, be prepared to stay behind it or get some very bad word-of-mouth publicity in your community. Conversely, if you do stand behind your products, you'll get good word-of-mouth that will be invaluable, that you couldn't buy with advertising dollars.

Another kind of honest objection—though it's not always an honest objection—is the competitive objection. "I can get bigger ones for the same price down the street." "They give a better guarantee on the same goods out at the shopping plaza." "How come your prices are so high? I just got the same thing the other day for ten dollars less."

Maybe. Maybe not. Usually it just isn't so. When it's not an honest objection, it's often just talk aimed at exploring how firm your price policy is. When it is an honest objection, it's usually a misunderstanding or misconception on the part of the customer. Often the "same thing" turns out to be of lower quality; the better guarantee turns out to be not as good as the customer was told when you get down to the fine print.

Competitive objections are always to be handled calmly, courteously, and often with the reassurance that you stand ready to meet all competition.

And no matter what your customers say your competitors said about you, never attack your competitors in any way.

CONVINCE ME MORE

Customers are skeptical, and with good reason. No matter how ethical you are, you can assume that every single person coming through your door has had some pretty bad experiences with businesspeople who are a lot less ethical than you are. "He talks like a used-car salesman" slanders thousands of honest used-car salesmen, but unfortunately the slander has stuck, and not just to used-car salesmen but to all sellers.

The skeptical customer discounts much of what you say and a good deal of what you show, is looking for tricks and evasions and won't communicate any more than is absolutely necessary to get information on which to base a buying decision.

You're not going to change the skepticism a lifetime of experience has implanted. The best you can do is moderate it by being yourself. Once the skeptic gets to know you, has a few good experiences with you, you'll have a customer for as long as you're in business. At the start, though, be prepared to present and re-present, demonstrate and redemonstrate. Be prepared for all kinds of silly-sounding questions, aimed at trapping you into revealing your "true" attitudes.

The most difficult problem the skeptical customer poses is that you will often find it very hard to determine what the real objection to buying is. You'll need to question, to probe, sometimes to actually voice an objection yourself, to employ several techniques aimed at penetrating the skeptic's wall of resistance.

SMOKESCREENS

The skeptic and many other customers throw up smokescreens, objections that may seem real enough, but which often have literally nothing to do with the real reasons for not buying now.

Assume that you are selling washing machines. A woman comes in, walks toward your demonstration models, begins to look at them. Like most people, she looks at the price tags rather carefully. She seems to narrow her examination down to two machines, differing by a little over $75 in price.

After a few minutes more of careful scrutiny, with special attention to those price tags, she looks around for help. You arrive, and she asks you to tell her a little more about the more expensive machine, seems really interested in it. You present it, and everything goes very well. She has a few questions and doubts, and seems well satisfied by your answers.

Yet, when you begin closing, she expresses doubts about the ability of the machine to do what you say it will do. You represent, try to close again. She changes her ground, wonders if that particular brand of machine is the one she really wants, says she's heard some bad things about it.

You respond with the manufacturer's warranty, backed by your own good name and service organization, drive the point home with proof stories. It doesn't seem to take. She begins to back away from the whole situation, says perhaps she ought to think about it a little more, talk it over with her husband.

What has gone wrong? You begin to think back, to try to figure out where it went wrong, how you can make it right. Not so easy, with the customer headed out the door within the next sixty seconds.

The price tags. But she hasn't raised any kind of question about price. Pride?

"I wonder if you would consider a somewhat less expensive machine, Mrs. Jones. We have one that does every major thing this machine will do, but costs $75 less. In fact, I saw you looking at it a little while ago. Would you like to take another look?"

"If you mean the one over by the door, yes, it did look nice. But it didn't have the kind of short, gentle cycle I need for my wash-and-wear things."

"Oh, I see. Actually, Mrs. Jones, all our machines handle wash-and-wear clothes, and very well indeed. It's just a question of some doing it differently from others. If you'll step over there, I'll be glad to show you how that machine does it."

You'll make the sale now. You've seen and correctly diagnosed a smokescreen of specific-seeming objections, reached into your observations and experience to come up with the real objection, answered that objection by stepping down to a less expensive model. Caution—be sure that the machine will do what you say it will do, or you'll find yourself with a returned machine on your hands and some bad word-of-mouth in the community.

It isn't always that easy. And you aren't always that quick. But once you start looking for hidden objections, and do it consistently, it gets a lot easier.

Beware the very real customer problem or reservation that you treat as a smokescreen. For example, some women, not many, still do have to consult their husbands on major purchases. Never treat the expressed objection lightly, but do make a habit of trying to find out how real it is and reaching through it if it's a smokescreen.

OBVIOUS EVASIONS

The customer who comes, looks around, then puts you off, when you approach, with "I'm just looking," may not want to get into a selling situation with you, using the obvious evasion. That's handled by reapproach, which sometimes moves into a presentation, sometimes not.

There's another kind of obvious evasion, however, that is a great deal more troubling. Some customers move into the selling situation, go through the whole presentation with you, sometimes ask questions during the course of the presentation, and then say something like "That's interesting. I'll think it over and get back to you," "Thanks. I'll talk it over with my wife and let you know," or "Not right now, thanks. Maybe later on." No smokescreen, no real objections, just a polite stall and no sale.

Like the smokescreen, this reaction usually hides a very real set of objections to buying now. Again, if you want to have any chance of making the sale, you'll need to reach back into observation of this particular customer and your general experience to try to reach through the stall to the real objections.

TWELVE

Making the Sale

*Hard or Soft Sell? / The Ultimate Test of Empathy /
You Can Be Your Own Worst Enemy / The Right Moment
To Close / Closing Attitudes / Focusing on Merchandise
Choices / Moving from the Objection into the Close /
Asking the Customer To Buy Now*

A FTER ALL IS SAID AND DONE, YOU'RE EITHER GOING TO close the sale or you're not. That's what it all adds up to, the bottom line, the difference between success and failure.

Putting it a little differently, we've discussed a good many hurdles on the way to the sale. Now it's time to discuss the final hurdle—closing the sale.

HARD OR SOFT SELL?

A great deal of nonsense has been written and taught about the "hard sell" and the "soft sell," about the various closing techniques and subtechniques.

The essence of closing, both for you and for your customer, lies in what has gone before. Certainly there are techniques that can be helpful in moving people to a buying decision, but in the main if it has gone well before your closing attempts, it will go well when you are closing. If it has gone badly before, no amount of technique can help you.

THE ULTIMATE TEST OF EMPATHY

"When should I try to close?" asks the inexperienced seller.

The answer seems a little unfair. It's that in the deepest sense you begin to make the sale on first contact with the customer, and you begin to be able to close when you've put yourself in the customer's shoes, have begun to be able to empathize with the customer's wants and needs.

Closing is the best test of empathy. If you have stayed with the customer all the way, understood and sold to wants and needs, it will be perfectly natural for you to consummate the sale, equally natural for you to regard the customer's questions, stalls, and objections as nothing but steps on the way to the sale, to be handled by your product knowledge and selling skills.

On the other hand, if you've lost your customer and don't know it, or perhaps never even established real contact with that customer, it will feel entirely unnatural to try to close, whenever you try, no matter how often you try.

YOU CAN BE YOUR OWN WORST ENEMY

In selling, and especially in closing, you can be your own worst enemy.

Nobody likes to be rejected. Sellers are rejected again and again. When you try to sell to customers, you invest more than time in that attempt—you invest something of yourself in the whole process. And no matter how well you know that a "won't buy now" decision is no personal reflection on you, enough such decisions have an emotional impact.

All sellers at one time or another react negatively to that feeling of multiple rejection, no matter how they try to avoid that reaction, and no matter how funny and pathetic the reaction seems to them in more rational moments. It's perfectly natural.

And it's equally natural for many sellers to develop a gun-shy reaction to selling, especially to asking for the order. The anticipated rejection becomes a powerful factor in such a seller's thinking and causes a great deal of closing failure.

Lack of empathy is an equally powerful factor. Sellers who stumble over objections, who worry about which is the right moment to close, who feel that if one opportunity is lost all is lost, are often people who simply don't know where their customers are in the selling process, how their customers feel about them and about what they're selling.

Occasionally, people selling in small businesses feel that selling hard and effectively is not the right tactic for them, that it conflicts with the business image they are striving to build. Fair enough, if that's the real reason, rather than a rationalization for unwillingness to sell hard because selling is somehow unclean and beneath them. That's usually a self-selecting attitude, though. The small business owner who feels that way usually moves the business into bankruptcy soon enough, and then doesn't have to worry about selling any more.

THE RIGHT MOMENT TO CLOSE

There isn't any right moment to close. Closing is a positive state of mind that starts with first contact. If you don't have real contact with the customer, every moment is wrong. If you do, there's nothing wrong with trying to close six or seven times in the course of one selling process.

You can tell when the customer is developing strong interest. The customer communicates with face, body, and voice, just as you do. Watch for both overt and unconscious signs of growing interest in you and in what you're selling.

Unless the customer is trying very hard to mask reactions, interest will show in the eyes. They will focus on you and on what you're showing and telling about, will widen and narrow responsively as you talk. Watch the hands—they will open, move just a little with yours as you gesture. Look for the involuntary nod of the head as you make a telling point—but beware the head that nods every step of the way; it may not mean agreement at all, but just be a defensive reflex. Look at the set of the whole body— leaning forward with interest or standing back with arms folded?

Look for the tone in which questions are asked, comments and objections voiced. Wary, tight voice, or easy, responsive, warm? There's a world of difference between the noncommittal, dry "Yes" and the growingly enthusiastic "Yes!"

There are some very obvious things a customer will say that will tell you to close the sale now. Often, their worth as closing indicators depends on when and how they are said.

For example, questions on installation and service occurring during or immediately following your product presentation may or may not be closing indicators. They are more likely to be questions or objections. On the other hand, those kinds of questions a little further down the line, when you think the customer is getting ready to make a buying decision, are clear-as-crystal signals that the customer is ready to buy now.

Closing indicators are seldom a matter of what words are said. They are much more often words said with a certain attitude that tells you it's time to make the sale now. Service, credit terms, price are only a few of the signals that sometimes can be objections and sometimes closing indicators. "How much did you say this costs?" can be a customer shocked at the cost of an item and putting a huge barrier in the path of the sale—or it can be the delighted comment of a customer who is ready to buy now.

CLOSING ATTITUDES

You know that if you can understand your customer's wants and needs, and convince that customer you can fulfill those wants and needs with your merchandise, you'll close the sale.

You'll close the sale. It's as simple as that. Your basic attitude has to be that it is purely a matter of fitting what you have to your customer's wants and needs. To sell successfully, you must believe that and project that belief to your customer by your every attitude and action. It's not a question of whether you'll close the sale, but of when.

It's often called "assuming sale," and, if it is your real attitude, can be the most powerful single sales tool you possess.

People tend to move along with you in whatever direction you go strongly enough. That's why another important closing attitude is that of affirmation. It's sometimes described as keeping everything "upbeat," and when done in an insincere, excessively syrupy way is a proper subject for caricature.

All it really means, all you need to do, is to keep any negatives out of the selling situation. When people are thinking positively, they're thinking "yes." When thinking negatively, they're thinking "no." You want a "yes" for your product, want your customers to start saying "yes" and keep on saying it all the way through to the close of the sale.

Assume, for example, that you're selling tables. You say "Do you think this table is big enough to meet your needs?" The customer says "No." You say "Oh, well then, how about this one? Is it the right size?" "No." You may inject several no's into the selling situation just by asking the question badly.

Ask instead, "Which of these three tables seems closest to the size you had in mind?" You'll get a positive affirmation as to size, without running the risk of any unnecessary negatives at all. That will create an opportunity for further affirmation, or agreement between you and the customer, as you say, "Yes, that table will certainly seat the number of people you had in mind," while you and the customer both nod your heads. Which sets the stage for your next comments, about how fine a table it is, and how many you've sold to large families, and so on to the close.

FOCUSING ON MERCHANDISE CHOICES

Quite early in the selling process, you begin to focus on those items the customer seems most interested in.

Perhaps the customer wants to look at window coverings, and you show blinds, shades, curtains, draperies—your whole line of window coverings. Pretty soon, you've got it down to a single kind or single combination of window coverings, and are presenting those choices that most closely seem to meet the customer's wants and needs and are most likely to get a favorable buying decision.

It often happens that later on, while handling objections and reviewing benefits, a number of other choices are revived. You can find yourself in the unhappy position of the fabric seller surrounded by twenty-five different samples, with a perplexed customer ready to give up and go out the front door, leaving the seller wondering what went wrong.

Failure to properly handle the question of choice is what went wrong. Throughout the selling process, you are developing merchandise choices in the most positive way possible, moving to define choices. Ideally, you come to the close with a single choice, on which you and the customer will agree.

The process of focusing choices is an essential part of the selling process, and a crucial aspect of the service you are rendering. Like the "answer man," you are holding yourself, quite properly, as an expert who will help your customer solve problems, select alternatives, make merchandise choices.

As an experienced seller, you'll stop just short of making the customer's choice. It's very tempting to fall into the trap of responding to the earnest question "Which one would you buy if you were in my shoes?'' without recognizing that question for the trap it is. People often take home merchandise they loved in the store, then change their minds. Then they blame you for selling them the merchandise. Your role is to help them right up to the choice; to state, restate, and emphasize the qualities and benefits of the merchandise; and to push them eventually to choose and make the purchase. The customer has to do the ultimate choosing.

MOVING FROM THE OBJECTION INTO THE CLOSE

There comes a time in every selling process when you are going to start asking the customer to make the buying decision now. There are a number of ways of doing it. You may use several different ways in a single selling situation, and without fear of antagonizing your customer.

Most often, it seems right to close the sale around your successful handling of an objection. There's no better time to close than when you and your customer have just agreed that your lawn mower isn't too expensive at all, but surprisingly low-priced in view of its quality and the number of things it will do for your customer. Then it's often a matter of saying "Fine, Mr. Smith. Will that be cash or charge?" If Mr. Smith isn't ready to buy, he'll tell, and without resentment. People are quite used to being asked for the order.

There is an often-used way of moving from the objection to the close which we strongly recommend you stay away from. It's called the "trap" close, which is what it is—a way of trapping your customer into making a buying decision.

Assume that you're selling lamps. You've shown several different styles, and at a point fairly well along in the selling process, the customer says "What I'd really like to see is one like that, but in an antique finish."

You know you have one. You pause, look serious, say "If I could get you a lamp like that, at the same price as this one, would you buy it?"

Without thinking very hard about it, the customer responds "Yes."

Aha. You've trapped the customer. You go through the motions of searching for it, pull out the lamp, start writing up the order.

Don't do it. Even if the customer buys, which is unlikely in this era of skeptical consumers, you may never see that customer again. And the word will soon enough get around that you're someone to be avoided.

People hate to think they've been had by a slick seller. You may legitimately feel that the "trap" close is an acceptable way of getting a procrastinating customer to make an overdue buying decision, but the customer is very likely to regard it as a low blow.

ASKING THE CUSTOMER TO BUY NOW

There are several ways of asking the customer to buy now.

You can assume sale.

All during the selling process, you have assumed that the customer will buy what you're selling. Now, at the close, it is perfectly natural to keep right on assuming that.

"Yes, Mr. Smith, that suit really does look good on you. Let's go on over to the fitting room and see what alterations need to be done." And you start moving in that direction.

"Good, Mrs. Jones. Will you take it with you, or do you want it sent?"

"Good choice. Will that be cash or charge?"

All of the above assume that the sale is made without forcing the customer to say "Okay, I'll take it."

No matter how well convinced your customer is, no matter how well you've moved up to the close, there is always a final barrier to be hurdled at the actual point of close. Making an overt buying decision requires an act of will, of consciousness. It is always easier for you and the customer if you can find a way to let the decision be made without a sharp, conscious act of will, but rather by letting the logic of the situation move along.

It's not a matter of fooling or trapping the customer into a buying decision. If you assume sale when the assumption is premature or just plain wrong, the customer will let you know soon enough that you haven't made the sale. And if you try assuming in an obviously manipulative way, you can destroy your credibility, and with it the sale you've worked so hard to make. But if you assume sale when it's logical and feels right to both of you, it's one of the best ways to close.

You can close on a small choice.
This is another good way of focusing on something other than the actual buying decision hurdle. It's really a way of assuming sale, but with a special aspect.

"Yes, that's a very fine radio. Do you want it in black or tan?"

"Those are our finest linen handkerchiefs. They come in boxes of a dozen each. Will one dozen be enough, or would you prefer two dozen?"

There are many small choices to be made by the customer after the sale has been consummated: the choices vary with the products bought. Closing on a small choice is an excellent way to go around, rather than directly over, the buying decision hurdle.

You can close on a method of payment.
Another special way of assuming sale while focusing on a small choice is "Will that be cash or charge?"

It's special, and very widely used, because it adds a final objection-handling comment to the selling process, right at the point of closing.

Many customers come through the whole selling process with price and money reservations firmly imbedded in their minds. Reservations, not the kinds of objections you have already handled. A customer may be quite convinced that your product is properly priced and affordable, and still come to the close with lingering, unexpressed, often subconscious doubts about the wisdom of the purchase.

"Will that be cash or charge?" tends to defuse that potential last-minute stumbling block to closing the sale. It reminds the customer that the purchase need not be paid for right now, that payment can be stretched out by use of one or another credit device. Putting it differently, it eases the pain of paying while still providing the gratification of product ownership and use right now.

You can close "on approval."

This is a weak way of selling, and usually causes more headaches than it's worth.

You're not actually saying "Take this home and try it" when you sell this way, but you might as well be doing just that.

This closing technique consists of not very subtly stressing your return policies and guarantees, and in effect issuing an open invitation to return merchandise if the customer isn't satisfied.

"We guarantee complete satisfaction or your money back."

"Let me tell you, Mr. Smith, we want completely satisfied customers. If, after using it for a few days, you're in any way dissatisfied, you just come back to see me, and I'm sure we can fix you up."

It's the sort of thing that gives selling a bad name. People are getting better and better informed about these kinds of selling tactics, and consumers have more and more legal protection in these areas.

No reputable small business can stay in business selling "on approval," and both customers and business owners know that very well.

You can close on a bargain basis.

"This item is on sale now. They're going fast, and in fact we don't have all sizes and styles in stock any more. If you want that one, you can have it, but I can't guarantee that I'll have it tomorrow."

"We have a special on these right now. They're going back to their regular price next week."

Bargain-basis closing is a very straightforward, widely accepted closing mode. As long as it's true. Small businesses can't afford to lose their credibility in the price area.

Beware the business impact of bargain-basis closing. The small business owner who does too much of it is liable to find profits shrinking alarmingly even while grosses rise. If you do offer specials, be sure to offer them for very limited times, on items that aren't moving well or on which you have big margins, and that they're producing the additional business you're hoping for.

A variation on bargain-basis closing is the "rising prices" close. Just be sure that prices really are going up.

You can close on a "get on board" basis.

This is often a combination of "We're selling an awful lot of these this year" and "We're running out of stock on these. Don't know when we're going to get any more in; factory can't seem to supply enough to meet the demand. Joe, do we have any more of these cast-iron widgets in stock out back, or is this the last one?"

Don't use this one. Even if it's true, and no one for a hundred miles around has any more cast-iron widgets, the customer is likely to think you're pulling one of the oldest tricks in the book, and may be insulted enough to go right out the front door and not come back again.

You can close by asking for the order very directly.

Sometimes, and especially when what is being bought requires writing up a fairly complicated sales slip and the signature of the customer, you will want to simply ask for the order. It may be as simple as writing up the slip as you talk with the customer, then handing the customer the filled-in sales slip and saying "Fine. Will you please put your name right there?"

You may want to develop your whole close around the sales slip, asking for the customer's name and how it's spelled, address, raising choice questions, quoting prices and putting them into the sales slip, while you continue responding to the customer's questions and objections. It's another way of assuming sale; it ends with you asking for the customer's name on the sales slip. Note that you don't ask for the customer's signature. That sounds somehow too legal and formal, like a contract. You ask the customer to "please put your name here," which is considerably less forbidding and makes the decision seem more routine.

Silence is not a very good way of asking for the order in a small business selling situation. It's a useful closing pressure technique in industrial selling, but in most small business situations the odds in favor of interruption just when you think your customer has decided to buy are too great.

After the Sale

WHAT YOU MAKE HAPPEN AFTER THE SALE CAN SPELL THE difference between business success and business failure, between substantial overall profits and disappointingly marginal results.

In today's economic climate, and given the very heavy competition faced by all small business owners, your profit margins are under continuing attack. On many items in stock, you are forced to sell at prices that are at best minimally profitable, in the hope that you will stimulate traffic, develop repeat business, and be able to use your selling skills to move more profitable items once you have people to sell to.

Your main edge is you, and that is never more apparent than in the area of what to do after the sale is made.

The discount store customer walks in, often makes a yes-or-no buying decision without any assistance, goes to the checkout counter, and pays for the merchandise. With luck, the checkout clerk says "Thank you."

In many department stores, the customer gets help, makes a buying decision, pays for the item, and leaves. Sometimes the clerk says "Will there be anything else?"

Alert, skilled small business owners do it a little differently. They know that adding related items, selling larger quantities, selling up to higher quality and price, getting started on the repeat items in a sale, moving on to other kinds of items, and starting a sound service relationship all add up to building profits now and to long-term customer relationships that will yield many kinds of business-building benefits over the years.

SELLING RELATED ITEMS

"Will there be anything else?" no matter how nicely said, often calls forth an immediate "No, thank you." And that's that. One sale made, all other opportunities blown, and the customer out the door.

"That's a lovely blouse. I think one of these scarves might go extremely well with it. We just got them in yesterday. Here, why don't you see how this one looks?"

"I think you've made a fine choice, Mr. Smith. Those shoes are lightweight, sturdy, and will last you a long time. By the way, I'd like you to take a look at the lightweight rubbers on the table behind you. They weigh just a few ounces and fold right up into their own little carrying case. You can put them in your briefcase on a cloudy morning, wear them home if it rains. And shoes as good as the ones you buy deserve protection against the elements. Here, let me show you a pair."

There are all kinds of items you can relate to purchases just made, and doing that kind of relating and selling is one of the most profitable habits you can develop. The cheese store owner sells cookies and breads. The lamp seller can supply half a dozen special bulbs so that you have a stock on hand. The automobile dealer sells a car stereo as an "option."

The key to all add-on sales lies in the relationship you've developed with the customer by the time you've closed the original sale. At precisely that point, your stock is usually very high indeed with your customer. The buying decision has been made, you've offered congratulations on the excellence of the choice, and you, as trusted adviser, can reasonably be expected to offer suggestions aimed at satisfying other customer wants and needs.

Timing is important. The right time is when the original sale has been closed, but before the sales slip has been completed, the register rung, or an item wrapped or otherwise prepared for removal from the premises. Once any of those things has occurred, the transaction between you and your customer has been completed, and any additional sales are new transactions in the customer's mind. You have the customer's full attention between the close of the original sale and the completion of the mechanics of that sale; you will make add-on sales best in that period.

Suggestion is crucial. This is the best time to use a variation of the "merchandise opening," which we don't recommend as a first contact device (see Chapter Eight). In the add-on sale situation, the merchandise approach puts you in motion and allows you to show and sell to an entirely sympathetic customer, with very little chance of causing antagonism on the customer's part.

SELLING UP

Substitution is the underlying process going on when you are "selling up"—that is, selling higher-quality, usually higher-priced merchandise to a customer who has expressed specific interest in a lower-priced item by brand name or price range.

The simplest and most common form of substitution occurs when someone comes in and asks for something you either don't stock at all or on which you're temporarily out of stock.

If you're out of stock, the customer is someone you know, and the item can't be bought for a quarter across the street, you'll probably try to hurry the reorder, and ask the customer to wait for the reorder to come in if possible.

More often, you'll say something like "We don't have it by that particular name, but I think we have something that will do exactly the same thing."

You're unlikely to commit any of the classic errors of the inexperienced clerk: "No. We don't carry those. Had them for a while, but they didn't move. You might try the five-and-ten." Or "No, but we have something just as good." A little better than the first, but not much. That rejoinder is almost guaranteed to make the customer get set for a high-pressure sell of inferior merchandise.

As in all selling situations, your main effort is to tie you and your merchandise to your customer's wants and needs. People stick to brands or exact prices quoted very rarely, will usually respond reasonably to your attempt to meet their needs with other merchandise.

"Selling up" can happen at the start, as when your suggested merchandise is somewhat more expensive than the merchandise originally requested by the customer. In general, it's best to try to find out what the customer hopes to get from the product, responding with higher-priced merchandise if necessary, rather than responding on price alone. If the customer has seen a self-propelled lawn mower advertised somewhere for $150, and your least expensive self-propelled mower is $200, show that, rather than showing a manually propelled mower at $150. You can always come down to the lower price; you may lose the customer immediately if you don't show the functions wanted.

At almost any time during the selling process, you may decide to change ground and try to sell more expensive merchandise. It usually gets harder to do as you get further along, is usually easiest when beginning to develop customer choices.

"Hello, I want to try on a pair of the cloth-covered casual shoes you have near the front of your window display. They cost $14.95 and the style number is 02237. I'm a size 10D."

"Fine. Won't you sit right here, sir? I'll get some for you to try on. Will you be using them outdoors a good deal?"

"Yes. They look nice and light."

"They are, and very good for that purpose. At the same time, though, let me show you another shoe that you might like even more. It's a little more expensive, but we find that it lasts so much longer outdoors because of the specially processed top and waterproofing that it actually saves you money in the long run. Either one will do the job for you, of course."

"Okay, let's see them both."

Given that kind of approach, the customer will almost always display an open mind. Note very carefully that you haven't in any way downgraded his original choice. That's crucially important if you want to bring the sale to a successful conclusion. Never attack your customer's judgment or suggest that the original choice was cheap or in any way shoddy.

You can also "sell up" in a very long-range way, as does the automobile dealer who starts a young customer with the least expensive model in stock and moves the customer over the years to the top of the line.

SELLING LARGER QUANTITIES

The basic larger quantity add-on is a great deal like the small choice close. You've sold a can of mildew remover, say "Might it be useful to take three cans instead of one? That way you can keep one upstairs, one downstairs, and hold one in reserve. And it will save you a trip back. Besides, they're three for five dollars, two dollars a can. You save a dollar."

Everybody wants to save a dollar, if it makes sense. And the way the mildew remover add-on sale was presented does make sense. Mildew often returns, and your customer is quite likely to use three cans within a reasonable time.

The key elements are usually convenience and price, though sometimes you'll do it on one or the other alone. On some very small items, the money decision isn't much of a factor, but not having to make a trip back to restock may be.

Quantity add-on sales can be an important element in your profit picture. Those smallish items which best lend themselves to this technique are often items on which you make relatively high per-unit profits, and increased volume can mean significantly increased profits.

SELLING REPEAT ITEMS

Some products have built-in repeat sales. For example, battery-operated toys are sold once and create a continuing need for replacement batteries. Some kinds of coffee-making machines create a need for disposable strainers that fit into the machines. Some kinds of pens require replacement cartridges.

You can and should sell replacement items as add-ons directly after the close on the original item sold. It's especially useful for the customer to have extras when the replacement parts fit only the items purchased. Then the replacement parts are a valuable customer service, and the customer regards you as the source of supply right from the start. That means repeat business and possible future sales of other items to the same customer.

SELLING OTHER KINDS OF MERCHANDISE

You will often find it possible to move on to the sale of entirely unrelated items.

One way of doing that is to be attentive during the selling process to any clues you may pick up as to other customer wants and needs. That's one of the best reasons for being entirely alert and carefully watchful from the moment the customer comes in. The customer who stops and studies the silverware before moving on to eventually buy a hair-dryer may walk out with both, if you're observant and skillful. The customer who buys a snowblower one cold December morning may also buy that set of golf clubs you so hopefully have on sale.

Another approach is to use new or seasonal items as interest-arousers.

"Have you seen our new line of sportswear?"

"We just got our ski equipment line in for the winter season."

"We're handling the Wiggins line of kitchenware now, and I know you're always on the lookout for new and interesting casserole dishes. They have two that I think are outstanding. Let me show them to you." And you're in motion.

The bargain approach is another tried and true way of moving to sale of unrelated items. People may or may not buy, but hardly anyone will resent being told of an authentic limited-term price reduction.

"While you're in, Mrs. Smith, let me mention that we're having our annual midwinter sale of golfing equipment. We're featuring as much as 30 percent off on some of the best brand-names in the field."

EXTRA CHARGES

Very few customers are surprised by extra charges for deliveries, especially deliveries of large items. They know that you, as a small business owner, probably have to make outside arrangements for deliveries and installations.

What can cause a lot of trouble, though, is surprising your customer with those extra charges. At the point that you are saying "Will you take it with you or do you want it sent?" you'd better be sure to tell the customer about any delivery charges. You can soften the impact of delivery and installation charges by pointing out money savings if the customer takes the item along, and on large items if the customer handles the installation. Instead of saying "If you want it delivered, it will cost you an extra $5," why not say "If you take it with you, you can save the $5 delivery charge."

Gift wrapping is another area of potential trouble. Department stores hardly ever gift wrap free any more. Why should you? Customers usually understand that you can't. But don't surprise them. If there are extra charges for gift wrapping, say so while you're completing the order.

Service contracts on large items such as appliances should always be gone over very carefully with the customer, so that you are sure the customer fully understands all charges and all services rendered under the service contract.

Warranties should also be gone over very carefully. The customer should fully understand when you will do repairs under warranty, when the manufacturer will do the repairs, for how long, and to what extent. Many warranties, for example, call for parts to be supplied free by the manufacturer for a reasonably long period, but labor to be supplied free for a much shorter period. As a practical matter, that may mean a bill for labor when the customer thinks the item is still fully covered by warranty. The last thing in the world you want to confront is an angry customer claiming that you were tricky with the fine print in the warranty.

Sometimes going out of your way to provide customer service can boomerang, if you're not careful. For example, you may put in a very special rush order for a single item to provide one of your customers with a much-desired product. You may also fail to make it clear that there will be a special shipping charge to airmail the item from the factory a thousand miles away. Then, when you triumphantly present the item to your customer, you can find yourself in an annoying and entirely unnecessary dispute over the airmail charges.

SERVICE

Service is part of selling. It keeps the currently made sale solid, reduces complaints and returns, provides the basis for long and profitable customer relations.

Service is also expensive, and getting more expensive all the time. You have to charge for it, and it's the rare small business that makes money on its service operations.

But service is one of the most important competitive tools you have. You can often be undersold by discount operations. People come to you, become your customers, partly because they know they can rely on you to stand behind what you sell. The truth is that service is an essential aspect of most small businesses. And if you need to give service, let it be the best possible.

An extraordinarily important part of service is simply showing your customers that you care about them after they make the purchase.

It can be as little a thing as having someone help a customer out to the car with a heavy item.

It can and should be a call from you to someone who has bought a substantial item that had to be delivered and installed to make sure that everything went well and that all is in working order. Surprisingly, very few small business owners do that, even though a two-minute call may forestall time-consuming complaints and pave the way for additional hundreds of dollars' worth of business in the future.

Some small business owners make a practice of dropping notes to their customers after substantial purchases, thanking them for their patronage. It's casting bread upon the waters, and it works.

Your customers will understand that you have to charge for service, whether in the form of a service contract or directly for the work performed. In fact, service is so important that many purely service operations have branched out, successfully put in lines of new equipment, then sold and serviced their own sales. Similarly, some small businesses have put in service operations, been able to price those services so that they were at least self-sustaining, and found themselves profitably servicing a great deal more than their own sales. The hidden profit often is that when you service an item bought from someone else, the customer comes to you to buy new when it's time to replace the item you've been servicing.

LAYING THE GROUNDWORK FOR FUTURE SALES

There are two essential things you want after the current sale and possible add-ons have been completed.

First, you want your customer's okay to mail sales material from time to time. The way to handle this is to say something like "Mrs. Smith, we have special sales, new lines, things happening from time to time during the year that I'd like to let you know about. Will it be all right with you if we mail you information now and then?" Perhaps one in a thousand customers will say no. Most of the others will be surprised that you even ask, but will appreciate being asked.

Second, you want your customer's okay to call now and then on items you think will be of interest. Again, you should not have any difficulty in getting that okay.

CONCLUSION

Strong motivation and seasoned selling skills are essential success ingredients for small business owners. Nobody but you can supply motivation. We hope that this book has helped you to further develop your selling skills.

Suggested Reading

Beach, Frederic A., Frank H. Beach, and Richard H. Buskirk, *Textbook of Salesmanship* (New York: McGraw-Hill, 1974).

Bodle, Yvonne G., and Joseph A. Corey, *Retail Selling* (New York: McGraw-Hill, 1972).

Crissy, William J., and William H. Cunningham, *Effective Selling: A Short Course for Professionals* (New York: Wiley, 1977).

Harding, Jack, *Retail Selling Is Fun* (Danville, Ill.: Interstate, 1970).

Hoyt, Homer, *People, Profits, Places: A Blueprint for Retailing* (New York: National Retail Merchants Assn., 1969).

James, Don L., *Retailing Today* (New York: Harcourt Brace Jovanovich, 1975).

Lee, J. E., *Five Basic Steps in Planned Retail Selling* (Elmsford, N.Y.: Pergamon Press, 1970).

Loffel, Egon W., *Financing Your Business* (New York: Wiley, 1977).

Richards, Gerald F., *Tax Planning Opportunities* (New York: Wiley, 1977).

Robinson, O. Preston, Christine H. Robinson, and George H. Zeiss, *Successful Retail Salesmanship* (Englewood Cliffs, N.J.: Prentice-Hall, 1961).

Seder, John W., *Credit and Collections* (New York: Wiley, 1977).

Telchin, Charles F., and Seymour Helfant, *Planning Your Store for Maximum Sale and Profits* (New York: National Retail Merchants Assn., 1975).

INDEX

111